FLEX APPEAL

NAVIGATING THE NEW WORLD OF FLEXIBLE WORK. HOW TO BE SUCCESSFUL AND HAPPY.

DESMOND WINTERS

TABLE OF CONTENTS

Prologue	7
Introduction	9
1. THE FUNDAMENTALS OF FLEXIBLE WORK	13
1.1 The Evolution of Work: From Office-Bound to Digital Nomad	15
1.2 Current Landscape: From Perk to New Norm	16
1.3 Impact of Technology: Enabling the Shift Toward Flexible Work	20
1.4 Changing Workforce Expectations: Valuing Work-Life Balance Over Job Security	23
1.5 Challenges and Opportunities: Navigating Flexible Work Models	25
1.6 Future Outlook: How Flexible Work Will Evolve	27
1.7 The Gig Economy	29
2. PREPARING FOR THE TRANSITION	31
2.1 Assessing Your Readiness for Flexible Work	31
2.2 Setting Personal and Professional Goals	38
2.3 Navigating the Job Market for Flexible Roles	41
2.4 Negotiating Flexible Work Arrangements with Your Employer	45
2.5 The Mental Shift: Preparing for a New Way of Working	47

3. KEYS TO SUCCESS OF THE FLEXIBLE WORKER — 51
   3.1 Designing Your Ultimate Home Office — 51
   3.2 Time Management Techniques for the Flexible Worker — 55
   3.3 The Art of Minimizing Distractions and Procrastination — 58
   3.4 Establishing a Powerful Daily Routine — 61
   3.5 The Role of Physical Fitness in Enhancing Productivity — 64

4. MASTERING THE TOOLS OF THE TRADE — 69
   4.1 Communication Tools: Beyond Email and Zoom — 69
   4.2 Achieving Clarity in Virtual Communications — 73
   4.3 Staying Connected: Building Relationships in a Remote World — 76
   4.4 Protecting Your Data: Cybersecurity for the Home Worker — 79

5. BUILDING AND MANAGING REMOTE TEAMS — 83
   5.1 The Foundations of Trust in Remote Teams — 83
   5.2 Virtual Team-Building Activities That Work — 87
   5.3 Managing Cross-Cultural Remote Teams — 90
   5.4. The Remote Leader: Strategies for Inspiring Your Team — 94
   5.5 Performance Measurement and Feedback in a Flexible Team — 97

6. THE PERSONAL CHALLENGES OF FLEXIBLE WORK — 103
   6.1 Handling Feelings of Isolation and Loneliness — 103
   6.2 Drawing Boundaries: Work-Life Balance in Practice — 106

6.3 Dealing with Overwork and Burnout — 108
6.4 Overcoming Technological Overwhelm — 111
6.5 Navigating Career Progression Remotely — 114

7. YOUR MENTAL AND EMOTIONAL WELL-BEING — 117

7.1 The Psychology of Working Remotely — 117
7.2 Strategies for Managing Remote Work Anxiety — 120
7.3 The Impact of Physical Space on Mental Health — 124
7.4 Building a Support Network for Remote Work Success — 127

8. ADVANCING YOUR CAREER IN A FLEXIBLE WORLD — 131

8.1 Skill-Building and Continuous Learning from Home — 131
8.2 Networking and Collaboration in a Virtual World — 134
8.3 Personal Branding for the Remote Worker — 137
8.4 Finding and Securing Remote Work Opportunities — 140
8.5 Navigating Promotions and Raises as a Remote Employee — 143

9. FUTURE-PROOFING YOUR REMOTE WORK LIFE — 147

9.1 Anticipating and Adapting to Changes in Remote Work — 147
9.2 The Role of AI and Automation in Flexible Work — 148
9.3 Sustainable Remote Work Practices — 153
9.4 Balancing Flexibility with Security: Financial Planning for the Future — 154

10. **BEYOND THE HOME OFFICE** — 157
   10.1 Integrating Work and Life: A Holistic Approach — 157
   10.2 Hobbies and Interests: Recharging Outside Work Hours — 158
   10.3 Volunteering and Community Engagement as a Remote Worker — 159
   10.4 Physical Wellness and Nutrition for the Home-Based Worker — 160
   10.5 Planning for Time Off: Vacations and Staycations for the Flexible Worker — 162

11. **WORKING FROM HOME FOR PARENTS** — 165
   11.1 Benefits and Pitfalls — 165
   11.2. Challenges of Managing Different Age Groups — 167
   11.3 Tips for Parents Working from Home or Performing Hybrid Work — 169

Conclusion — 175
About the Author — 179

PROLOGUE

Over the past decade, the landscape of work has dramatically transformed. Technological advances, cultural shifts, and global events like the COVID-19 pandemic have accelerated the adoption of flexible work arrangements. High-speed internet, cloud computing, and collaborative tools have made remote work not just feasible but preferable for many. This shift has underscored the need for a comprehensive approach to managing flexible work that addresses personal and professional aspects.

My name is Desmond Winters, and I have spent the last six years as a business coach, with three years focusing on remote work environments. With a career spanning financial services, IT, construction, and education, I've experienced firsthand the growing need for adaptable work solutions. My passion for continuous learning and personal development drives me to share the insights and strategies I've gathered.

Embark on a journey with me to explore the myriad opportunities that flexible work offers. Together, we will confront its challenges and leverage its potential to cultivate a more harmonious, productive, and satisfying work life. Welcome to *Flex Appeal*.

INTRODUCTION

Today, flexible work has never been more appealing. The idea that we can unshackle ourselves from traditional 9-5 jobs and a daily grind to work anywhere, anytime, and on your terms is simply irresistible. The term "flexible work" is more than just a buzzword—it's a lifeline for all of us seeking balance, productivity, reward, and satisfaction in our careers. The rise of the gig economy is changing how companies hire employees and offers even more opportunities to work on your terms. If you're reading this, you might be curious about how flexible work can transform your life, or perhaps you're looking to refine your approach to this new working mode you've already embraced. Either way, you're in the right place.

Why This Book? This book results from my triumphs and trials in navigating various flexible work modes. It's intended to cater to your needs, helping you avoid many common pitfalls you encounter along the way and providing practical tips so you can capitalize on the many benefits and promises that flexible work offers. These benefits and promises that we all want make it so appealing, and hence, we have titled this book Flex Appeal: Navigating the New World of Flexible Work.

What to Expect Flex Appeal is your comprehensive guide to mastering the flexible work environment. Here's what we'll cover:

- The Fundamentals of Flexible Work: Demystify different flexible work modes and what they mean for you.
- Preparing for the Transition: Practical steps to ensure you're ready to make the jump.
- Keys to Success for the Flexible Worker: Thrive, not just survive in this new setting.
- Mastering the Tools of the Trade: Explore the essential tools you need and how to use them effectively.
- Building and Managing Remote Teams: For leaders, how to build, manage, and inspire your team.
- The Personal Challenges of Flexible Work: Overcoming some of the less-discussed challenges.
- Your Mental and Emotional Well-Being: Keeping your mind and spirit in optimal condition.
- Advancing Your Career in a Flexible Work Environment: Moving up without burning out.
- Future-Proofing Your Remote Work Life: Staying relevant in a rapidly changing world.
- Beyond the Home Office: Expanding your work life and environment.

Who Should Read This Book? Whether you're a seasoned telecommuter struggling to adapt to this "new" world of flexible work or need to maximize performance and productivity to move ahead, a manager overseeing a remote team, or someone just stepping into this new norm, this book offers tailored advice to enhance your experience and outcomes.

Why It Matters The shift toward flexible work arrangements has been on the horizon for many years and accelerated due to the COVID-19 pandemic. But these changes are here to stay. We must embrace these new everyday demands, adapt to new work modalities, and rethink how we define success and productivity.

How to Use This Book As a guidebook, you don't need to read this book from cover to cover. Browse the topics that most interest you or are seeking answers by browsing the contents page. Then, jump straight into those chapters that are relevant to you and look at the strategies and tips provided. You can always return to the other topics as you continue your journey.

The Benefits for You By the end of this book, you'll have a clear blueprint for

- Setting up a flexible work environment that fosters creativity and efficiency.
- Building resilience and strategic thinking within your new work paradigm.
- Enhancing your well-being and career prospects in ways that traditional roles often restrict.
- Managing people and teams effectively in this environment.

As we transition into the next chapter on The Fundamentals of Flexible Work, remember that each step forward is about crafting a work life that respects your personal life and aspirations. Together, we'll explore how flexible work can fit and enhance your current lifestyle, making you more fulfilled and, ultimately, more successful.

CHAPTER 1
THE FUNDAMENTALS OF FLEXIBLE WORK

If you asked ten people what "flexible work" means, you'd probably get ten different answers. The concept has grown increasingly popular but remains elusive because it's not a one-size-fits-all solution. Let's break down the fundamental modes and terminologies that form the backbone of flexible work, clarifying what these arrangements look like today and how they may shape our future.

Hybrid Work Hybrid work marries the best of both worlds: on-site and remote work. Employees split their time between the office and a remote location (often home), tailoring their schedule to their personal preferences or organizational requirements. **Example:** An employee might work in the office three days a week to attend important meetings and collaborate face-to-face but spend the remaining two days at home, avoiding long commutes and having fewer distractions to concentrate on focused tasks.

Telecommuting The employee works primarily from home through telecommuting but remains connected to their team through technology. This arrangement is usually location-independent, offering flexibility in working hours and style. **Example:** A software developer telecommutes daily, occasionally visiting the office for quarterly project reviews.

Remote Work Remote work takes telecommuting a step further. It's location-independent, meaning employees can work from anywhere with an internet connection. **Example:** A content writer works from a beachfront cafe while their employer is in a different city.

Part-Time Work Part-time work involves fewer hours than full-time work, usually offering fewer benefits but providing more personal time. **Example:** A customer support representative works four hours per day, five days a week, leaving their afternoons free.

Flextime Flextime allows employees to choose when they start and finish their workday within certain limits, offering a blend of structure and flexibility. **Example:** An accountant begins work at 7 a.m. to accommodate their early-morning productivity and ends early in the afternoon to pick up their children from school.

Job Sharing Job sharing allows two employees to share the responsibilities of one full-time role, effectively combining their talents and reducing individual workloads. **Example:** Two part-time marketing professionals alternate shifts throughout the week, sharing the workload so that their combined presence is equivalent to one full-time role.

Compressed Workweek A compressed workweek involves working the same hours as a standard week but over fewer days.

Example: An HR specialist works four ten-hour days per week, leaving them with a three-day weekend.

1.1 THE EVOLUTION OF WORK: FROM OFFICE-BOUND TO DIGITAL NOMAD

The transformation of the workplace from strictly office-bound environments to today's increasingly fluid work-from-anywhere culture is not just a change; it's a revolution. Understanding this shift requires looking back at where we started and appreciating how far we've come.

Historically, work was a place you went, not something you did remotely. The concept of the "9-to-5 job" in an office environment was the standard. This practice was based on industrial age principles, which stated that showing up at a specific location for a designated period was essential for oversight and productivity. Offices were designed to keep workers close to their tasks and each other, believing that physical presence facilitated better collaboration and faster problem-solving.

The emergence of the Internet and mobile computing throughout the 1980s and 1990s challenged the necessity of the traditional office. As technology advanced, so did the possibilities for communication and collaboration. Tools like email, video conferencing, and real-time collaborative platforms reduced the need for constant physical presence. Workers could now perform tasks and connect with colleagues from different locations and time zones, setting the stage for radical workplace transformations. Initially, workplace flexibility was limited to telecommuting a few days a week or using flextime to accommodate personal appointments. However, as technology continued to evolve and the workforce started demanding better work-life balance, companies began to see flexibility as a viable option. This shift was about employee satisfaction, tapping into a broader talent pool, and reducing overhead costs. Enter the era of digital nomads—individuals who use computer and telecommunications technologies to make their living nomadically. These professionals have pushed the boundaries of what it means to "go to work." Instead of being tied to a single location, digital nomads operate from coffee shops, co-working spaces, or exotic locales, often traveling while they work. The culture of working from anywhere has gained momentum, supported by a growing ecosystem of tools and services designed to facilitate remote work. Companies now offer location-independent positions, appealing to a generation that values flexibility, autonomy, and the integration of work into a lifestyle of travel and exploration.

1.2 CURRENT LANDSCAPE: FROM PERK TO NEW NORM

In the past, flexible work was seen as a unique perk offered sparingly to only a few privileged employees. It was reserved mainly for those in high-demand fields or people whose personal situations warranted special arrangements. Today, that landscape has shifted dramatically. Flexible work is no longer the exception; it is increasingly the rule, fundamentally changing how businesses operate and how people perceive their careers. Several European and Asian countries have already introduced policies to force companies and organizations to modify their work practices to accommodate flexible working arrangements. Since 2020, most workers in Finland can choose when and where they work for at least 50% of their working week. France, already famous for its 35-hour week, made it illegal for companies with more than 50 employees to contact their employees outside of working hours. Portugal has taken it even further - employers cannot contact employees after hours, cannot monitor employees working remotely, and must cover expenses incurred from working at home, such as internet and electricity. Portuguese parents can also work from home without prior arrangements with employers. Belgium has already introduced a 4-day week while other countries, like Spain, Iceland, UK and Japan, are trialing 4-day work weeks. By Dec 2024, Singapore will implement new guidelines requiring all employers to have formal processes for employees to request flexible work arrangements. However, these policies will continue to evolve and develop due to the many approaches to the scale, coverage, organization, and regulation of flexible working arrangements.

Early Adopters and Skepticism

Early adopters were often trailblazing tech companies or startups when remote work and other flexible arrangements started gaining traction. These businesses, recognizing the value of attracting top talent and reducing overhead costs, implemented flextime and telecommuting policies to lure skilled professionals tired of rigid office hours. Despite their initial success, skepticism abounded. Many traditional businesses questioned the productivity and accountability of remote workers. Could they be trusted to deliver results without direct oversight? Would they slack off in their pajamas?

The Tipping Point: COVID-19 and the Forced Experiment

The global COVID-19 pandemic upended this skepticism overnight. Almost instantly, businesses across the globe were forced into a massive work-from-home experiment. Companies had to minimize physical contact to comply with new health measures and shifted their operations to a virtual model. This change created a pool of workers who could now work from home and be paid for performing specific tasks, gigs, or freelancing. Even organizations that had resisted remote work found themselves pivoting quickly to ensure operations continued. Surprisingly, many businesses saw productivity remain stable or improve as employees adapted. The work-from-home experience revealed that workers could be trusted and productive outside traditional offices. While challenges like virtual collaboration and managing isolation persisted, organizations recognized the long-term potential of a flexible workforce.

The New Norm: Embracing Flexibility

Today, flexible work has become essential to the employment landscape. Here's how:

- **Broader Acceptance:** Remote work has become standard for many organizations, especially in industries where employees can perform their tasks remotely.
- **Hybrid Models:** Companies have adopted hybrid work arrangements that combine the best of both worlds, with employees balancing office and home.

- **Employee Expectations**: Job seekers now prioritize flexibility alongside traditional benefits, influencing company policies.
- **Rethinking Office Space:** Businesses have re-imagined office spaces as collaborative hubs rather than mandatory daily destinations, reducing real estate costs.

Key Benefits

- **Access to Talent**: Employers can tap into a global talent pool unhindered by geographical constraints.
- **Improved Productivity:** Many employees report higher productivity with fewer distractions at home.
- **Reduced Overhead Costs**: Companies save on office-related expenses like utilities and real estate.
- **Enhanced Work-Life Balance**: Employees experience better work-life integration, reducing burnout and turnover.

Challenges to Navigate

- **Maintaining Culture:** Building and sustaining a cohesive company culture across a distributed workforce is challenging.
- **Managing Performance**: Measuring performance based on output rather than hours worked requires a cultural shift.
- **Combating Isolation**: Workers may feel isolated and disconnected, impacting mental health and team cohesion.

Flexible work is now a norm that demands rethinking how companies engage with their employees and how people approach their careers. It's no longer just a perk; it's a strategic imperative that organizations must embrace to remain competitive in an increasingly dynamic, interconnected world.

1.3 IMPACT OF TECHNOLOGY: ENABLING THE SHIFT TOWARD FLEXIBLE WORK

At the heart of the shift towards flexible work lies a technological revolution. Advances in internet connectivity, cloud computing, and collaborative tools have fundamentally changed how and where we work. Without these innovations, flexible work would remain a distant dream. Let's explore how technology has enabled this transformation.

Internet Connectivity: The Digital Highway

The rise of high-speed internet has been a game-changer, providing the backbone for all other tools and practices in flexible work.

- **Broadband Access**: High-speed broadband connects workers from their homes to their colleagues worldwide, enabling real-time communication and efficient access to information.
- **Mobile Data Networks**: Smartphones and tablets with reliable data networks allow workers to work almost anywhere—whether at a cafe, in transit, or even on vacation.

Cloud Computing: Your Office Everywhere

Cloud computing has virtually eliminated the need to be physically present to access files or software.

- **File Sharing & Storage**: Tools like Google Workspace and Microsoft 365 allow seamless collaboration, file sharing, and storage, regardless of location.
- **Remote Servers**: Companies host their core software and databases in the cloud, making them accessible securely to remote employees.

Collaborative Tools: Staying in Sync

Collaboration is crucial in the workplace, and remote work demands tools that mimic in-person interactions.

- **Video Conferencing**: Zoom, Microsoft Teams, and Google Meet have become vital for meetings, project discussions, and even casual chats, helping remote workers feel connected.
- **Messaging Apps**: Slack, Microsoft Teams, and others enable instantaneous messaging, file sharing, and project updates, digitally providing the "water cooler" experience.
- **Project Management Software**: Platforms like Asana, Trello, and Jira help manage tasks, timelines, and responsibilities, ensuring that teams remain coordinated and meet deadlines.

Security and Privacy Tools: Keeping It Safe

The shift to flexible work has highlighted the need for secure communication and data handling.

- **Virtual Private Networks (VPNs)**: VPNs provide encrypted connections that keep data safe and maintain privacy when accessing company networks from different locations.
- Multi-Factor Authentication (MFA): Protects sensitive systems and data by requiring additional verification beyond passwords.

Productivity Tools: Making Work Easier

Applications that help with productivity have blossomed, catering to various needs.

- **Time Tracking**: Software like Clockify, Toggl, and Time Doctor tracks time spent on projects, ensuring efficient work and accountability.
- **Note-taking and Organization**: Notion and Evernote help keep notes, plans, and projects organized.
- **Transcription Software**: Software applications and add-ons like Otter.AI, rev.com, Fathom, and Trint take audio from your meetings, interviews, presentations, and other recordings to generate accurate transcripts within minutes. With AI-assisted transcription, these applications can also create summary notes quickly.

1.4 CHANGING WORKFORCE EXPECTATIONS: VALUING WORK-LIFE BALANCE OVER JOB SECURITY

Workforce expectations have significantly transformed over the past few decades. Employees increasingly prioritize work-life balance over the traditional markers of job security, such as a steady paycheck and long-term tenure with a single employer. Let's dive into what's driving these shifting priorities.

The Rise of Work-Life Balance

Once regarded as a secondary concern, work-life balance has moved to the forefront of workforce priorities, and for good reason. Here's why: **Stress and Burnout Awareness:** High-stress levels and burnout have become significant concerns, with research linking them to decreased productivity and adverse health effects. Employees recognize that a poor work-life balance can quickly lead to burnout, reducing job satisfaction and career longevity. **Generational Shifts**: Millennials and Gen Z, who comprise a significant part of the workforce, tend to value experiences and personal fulfillment over traditional notions of career success. They see work as just one component of a well-rounded life rather than the focal point.

Technological Enablement: Technology has enabled employees to work more efficiently and autonomously, making rigid work hours seem antiquated. Employees feel empowered to complete their tasks in ways that best fit their schedules.

Rethinking Job Security

Job security is no longer simply about staying employed. Employees are reevaluating what makes them feel secure in their roles:

- **Skill Development**: Workers prioritize developing new skills and staying adaptable over sticking with one company, knowing that a broader skill set makes them more employable.
- **Diverse Income Streams**: Side hustles and freelance work have gained popularity as employees seek to diversify where they derive their income and reduce dependence on a single employer.
- **Remote Opportunities**: Flexible work offers a sense of security by reducing dependence on a particular location, opening doors to opportunities with employers worldwide.

Employer Response to Changing Priorities

To retain talent and stay competitive, employers are adapting to these new expectations:

- **Flexibility as a Standard**: Companies now offer flexible schedules, hybrid work models, and four-day work weeks to accommodate varying needs.
- **Wellness Programs**: Mental health resources, gym memberships, and wellness allowances are becoming integral parts of benefits packages.

- **Learning and Development**: Employers invest in upskilling and career development to nurture a more resilient, knowledgeable workforce.

1.5 CHALLENGES AND OPPORTUNITIES: NAVIGATING FLEXIBLE WORK MODELS

The shift towards flexible work has been met with excitement and hesitation. While there's broad recognition of its benefits, societies worldwide face unique challenges as they adapt to these new models. However, within these challenges lie significant opportunities for innovation and inclusivity.

Primary Challenges

Digital Divide: Not all employees have the same access to high-speed internet or reliable technology, making it difficult for some to participate fully in remote work. Employees without the necessary resources can struggle with communication, productivity, and career advancement.

Maintaining Company Culture: Nurturing a strong corporate culture that aligns with organizational values is tougher with distributed teams. Teams may become siloed, reducing camaraderie and increasing feelings of isolation.

Overworking and Burnout: Without clear boundaries between work and personal life, some employees work longer hours, leading to stress and burnout. Poor work-life balance negatively affects health, productivity, and job satisfaction.

Management Adaptation: Managers accustomed to overseeing employees in person may need help to adapt to new performance metrics and remote supervision. Poor management can reduce team morale, productivity, and clarity.

Legal and Regulatory Issues: Tax implications, cross-border work rules, and data security regulations create a complex environment for managing remote work. Employers must navigate different jurisdictions and legal frameworks, increasing compliance risks.

Key Opportunities

Global Talent Pool: By embracing location-independent work, companies can tap into a global talent pool, finding the best candidates regardless of geography. This approach provides access to diverse perspectives and allows smaller companies to compete for top talent. **Cost Savings**: Remote and flexible work arrangements can reduce the need for office space and related overhead expenses. Organizations can reallocate these savings to employee benefits, training, or business growth initiatives. **Diversity and Inclusion**: Flexible work offers more opportunities for individuals who are caregivers, have disabilities, or live in remote areas to participate fully in the workforce. A more diverse workforce brings varied perspectives, fostering creativity and innovation. **Work-Life Balance**: Employers can improve employee satisfaction and productivity by offering flexible schedules and reducing turnover. Satisfied employees are often more engaged and contribute positively to the organizational culture. **Innovation in Collaboration Tools**: The shift to flexible work has accelerated the development of new digital collaboration tools, making remote teamwork smoother and more effective. These tools bridge gaps for distributed teams and enhance efficiency in traditional office settings.

1.6 FUTURE OUTLOOK: HOW FLEXIBLE WORK WILL EVOLVE

Predicting the future is challenging, but current trends and technological developments provide valuable insights into how flexible work might continue to evolve. As organizations adapt to the changing landscape, these predictions can help us envision a future that embraces innovation and inclusivity.

Hybrid Work as the New Standard

The hybrid work model, where employees split their time between the office and remote locations, is likely to become the norm.

- **Personalized Schedules**: Employees can design work schedules that fit their personal lives, coming into the office primarily for collaborative or strategic activities.
- **Dynamic Offices**: Offices will be re-imagined as collaborative hubs with creative spaces, meeting rooms, and technology for hybrid meetings.

Technology: Enhanced Connectivity and Collaboration

The continued evolution of technology will play a pivotal role in shaping how we work.

- **Virtual Reality (VR) and Augmented Reality (AR)**: VR and AR could simulate physical presence

in virtual meetings, allowing people to feel more connected despite geographical distances.
- **Artificial Intelligence (AI)**: AI will support more innovative scheduling, automate routine tasks, and personalize training, boosting productivity and skill development.
- **5G Connectivity**: Faster internet speeds allow seamless data streaming, making high-quality virtual meetings and real-time collaboration easier.

Decentralized Workforce: Global Teams and Diverse Talent

As geographic barriers dissolve, companies will have access to talent worldwide.

- **Global Collaboration**: Time zones become less complicated as companies develop round-the-clock teams that leverage time differences for continuous productivity.
- **Localized Talent Pools**: With location no longer a limiting factor, organizations can tap into new markets, opening doors to diverse talent and perspectives.

Inclusivity and Accessibility

Flexible work will continue to break down barriers to employment for historically marginalized groups.

- **Accessible Tools**: Collaboration tools will be designed with accessibility in mind, ensuring that all employees can contribute fully.
- **Neurodiversity**: Flexible work environments will accommodate varying work styles, allowing neurodiverse individuals to thrive.

Work-Life Integration and Well-Being

Work-life balance will evolve into work-life integration, where the two blend seamlessly.

- **Flexible Benefits**: Employers will offer flexible benefits, such as mental health resources, reimbursements for home office expenses, and paid time off to foster well-being.
- **Outcome-Based Evaluations**: Companies will measure performance based on results and productivity rather than hours logged, providing employees with more autonomy.

1.7 THE GIG ECONOMY

The gig economy is a vibrant and growing sector within flexible work arrangements. It allows individuals to engage in short-term, project-based tasks tailored to their schedules and lifestyle preferences. This work mode is characterized by its flexibility, variety, and the ability to choose from a wide range of tasks that align with one's skills and interests.

Ridesharing and Delivery Services Platforms like Uber, Lyft, DoorDash, Deliveroo, and Grubhub allow individuals to earn money by providing transportation or delivering food. These roles offer the flexibility to work during peak hours or when it suits the individual's schedule.

Freelance Platforms Websites such as Upwork, Fiverr, and Freelancer connect skilled professionals with clients looking for a wide range of services, from graphic design and writing to programming and virtual assistance. Freelancers can select projects that match their expertise and time availability.

Home and Personal Services Apps like TaskRabbit and Thumbtack enable people to offer home repairs, cleaning, or personal assistance services. These platforms allow workers to set their rates and availability, providing a highly customizable work experience.

Creative and Digital Work Content creators, photographers, and designers can leverage platforms like Etsy, YouTube, and Instagram to monetize their creative skills. These opportunities often start as side gigs but can grow into substantial sources of income.

Accommodation and Space Sharing Airbnb allows homeowners to rent out their properties or spare rooms to travelers. This can be particularly lucrative in popular tourist destinations or peak travel seasons.

By embracing the gig economy, flexible workers can be free to choose their projects, control their schedules, and explore diverse income streams. However, success in this sector requires strategic planning, continuous learning, and a proactive approach to managing one's career. The gig economy offers unparalleled flexibility and challenges workers to be self-reliant, innovative, and adaptable in a rapidly changing job market.

CHAPTER 2
PREPARING FOR THE TRANSITION

As we navigate the evolving world of flexible work, we must recognize that only some are suited for its challenges and rewards. Making a smooth transition requires reflection, goal-setting, and the right mindset. Here's how you can prepare yourself:

2.1 ASSESSING YOUR READINESS FOR FLEXIBLE WORK

Self-Evaluation: Understanding Your Suitability

Before jumping into a flexible work arrangement, it's essential to determine if you're truly ready. A flexible work environment requires a unique blend of personal discipline, communication skills, organizational ability, and technological proficiency. Here's how to evaluate yourself:

Personal Discipline

A flexible work environment often means fewer direct oversight mechanisms, so you must manage your time effectively.

- **Work Hours and Deadlines**: Can you establish regular work hours and deadlines without reminders?
- **Focus and Distractions**: Can you concentrate on tasks without becoming easily distracted?
- Self-motivation: Can you stay driven and engaged without daily face-to-face interactions with colleagues?

** Tips*

- Try working remotely for a day or two, and note how well you can maintain focus and productivity.
- Track how much time you spend on productive tasks versus distractions to assess your discipline levels.

Communication Skills

Clear communication is crucial in flexible work settings where team members rely heavily on digital communication.

- **Clarity:** Can you explain your thoughts, ideas, and project updates through emails and messaging apps?
- **Timeliness:** Are you prompt in responding to emails, messages, and meeting invites?
- **Listening:** Do you actively listen to others and ask

questions to clarify instructions or provide constructive feedback?

* Tips

- Review previous emails and messages to evaluate the clarity of your communication. Be honest in assessing yourself. Identify what improvements you need to make.
- Ask a trusted colleague or friend to give feedback on your communication style.

Organizational Skills

With flexible work often comes the responsibility of managing multiple projects, deadlines, and priorities.

- **Task Management:** Can you effectively prioritize tasks and keep track of deadlines?
- **Workspace Organization:** Is your workspace arranged in a way that minimizes distractions and optimizes productivity?
- **Documentation:** Do you maintain thorough notes and records to ensure all project details are well-documented?

* Tips

- Review your current task management system to see if it aligns with your priorities and productivity needs. Are you achieving the required outcomes?

- Organize your workspace and see if it helps boost your focus and efficiency. Refer to "Workspace Requirements" below.

Technological Proficiency

A certain level of tech-savviness is essential to thrive in a flexible work environment where digital tools are your primary means of collaboration.

- **Digital Tools**: Are you comfortable using video conferencing, messaging apps, and project management software?
- **Troubleshooting**: Can you handle basic technical issues independently, like managing connectivity problems or software updates?
- **Security Awareness**: Do you understand the basics of online security to protect your work data?

** Tips*

- Do research on industry apps and tools that flexible workers in your industry are using. Check out user reviews and assess the pros and cons. Does it suit your specific needs?
- Once you have trialed and installed your selected app or tool, test your proficiency by setting up mock scenarios such as video meetings or project boards.
- Learn basic troubleshooting steps, such as resetting your router or updating software, to avoid technical problems.

Self-Evaluation Recap

We've already discussed how to assess your personal discipline, communication skills, organizational ability, and technological proficiency. Next, consider your physical workspace, identify skill gaps, and prepare your mindset for the journey ahead.

Workspace Requirements

A productive, distraction-free workspace is essential for success in flexible work.

- **Dedicated Space**: Find a specific area at home dedicated solely to work. A dedicated space will help you maintain focus and signal to others that you're in "work mode."
- **Ergonomic Setup**: To avoid strain and fatigue, invest in a comfortable chair, a supportive desk, and accessories (keyboard, monitor, webcam, etc.).
- **Lighting and Ventilation**: Ensure your workspace is well-lit with natural light and has proper ventilation.
- **Minimize Distractions**: Remove non-work-related items that might distract you, and consider noise-canceling headphones if the environment is noisy.

** Tips*

- Experiment with different workspaces until you find one that best suits your needs.
- Set a clear boundary between your personal and work areas to prevent overlap.

- Communicate with family and friends when you are working to minimize disruptions throughout the day.

Identifying Skill Gaps

We have already discussed crucial skills to thrive in a flexible work setting. Here's how to identify and address them:

- **Technical Proficiency**: Are there tools, software, or platforms you're unfamiliar with that your role requires?
- **Project Management**: Are you well-versed in task prioritization, progress tracking, and meeting deadlines?
- **Soft Skills:** Do you need to improve in communication, time management, or adaptability?

⁎ Tips

- **Online Courses:** Platforms like Coursera, Udemy, and LinkedIn Learning offer various technical and soft skills courses.
- **Mentorship:** Connect with colleagues or industry experts who can provide guidance and share best practices.
- **Practice Projects:** Create small projects to practice new skills, applying theoretical knowledge to practical situations.

Mindset Shift

Adapting to a flexible work environment requires a specific mindset to ensure your success:

- **Self-motivation**: Cultivate intrinsic motivation by setting personal goals and celebrating small wins.
- **Resilience**: Prepare for challenges and setbacks by practicing resilience and learning from each experience.
- **Work-Life Integration**: Learn to harmonize work and life by establishing boundaries, finding time for personal activities, and knowing when to unplug.
- **Communication**: Be proactive in communicating with colleagues and supervisors. Share your availability and seek feedback to ensure alignment.

** Tips*

- Reflect on past experiences to identify what motivates or demotivates you and adjust your approach accordingly.
- Develop a daily routine that includes time for reflection, goal-setting, and personal wellness activities.

This self-evaluation process will help you gauge your readiness for flexible work. Honest reflection on personal discipline, communication, organization, and technology will allow you to identify areas of strength and those requiring improvement, setting you on a solid path toward success in this new work environment. However, preparing for flexible work requires more than just technical know-how. Creating a conducive workspace, identifying and addressing skill gaps, and cultivating the right mindset will prepare you for a rewarding and successful transition.

2.2 SETTING PERSONAL AND PROFESSIONAL GOALS

Goal Setting Principles

Cultivate self-motivation by setting personal goals and working towards them. Setting goals is crucial to succeeding in a flexible work environment, helping you clarify your priorities and measure your progress. The SMART framework—specific, Measurable, Achievable, Relevant, and Time-bound—can guide you in creating objectives that genuinely work for you.

- **Specific**: Define what you want to achieve. For instance, "Develop proficiency in the new project management software" is clearer than "Learn more about productivity tools."
- **Measurable**: Include metrics to track progress, such as completing a certification course or leading three projects successfully.
- **Achievable**: Set challenging yet feasible goals based on your current workload and capabilities.
- **Relevant:** Make sure your goals align with your professional and personal aspirations.
- **Time-bound**: To stay on track, attach a deadline to each goal. For example, "Finish the certification course in six weeks."

Example Goals Using the SMART Framework:

- "Complete an online course on digital marketing within three months to enhance my remote work skill set."
- "Lead and deliver two inter-department projects successfully by the end of this quarter to demonstrate my leadership capabilities."

Balancing Aspirations with Reality

Finding the right balance between your goals and the realities of work-life integration is crucial.

- **Understanding Priorities**: Identify what matters most to you and prioritize goals that reflect these values, whether related to career progression, personal growth, or well-being.
- **Time Management**: Recognize time limitations and avoid overloading yourself. Instead of tackling too many goals simultaneously, focus on a few high-impact ones.
- **Boundaries**: Clearly define when you work and rest or pursue personal interests, ensuring neither area is neglected.

Continuous Learning and Adaptation

In the rapidly evolving world of flexible work, continuous learning and adaptation are vital for staying relevant and achieving your goals.

- **Identify Skill Gaps**: Assess which skills you lack and would need to achieve your goals or advance in your career.
- **Seek Development Opportunities**: Use online courses, workshops, and webinars to gain new knowledge and skills.
- **Adaptability**: Stay open to change and regularly reassess your goals to remain relevant in the changing landscape.

Measuring Success

Tracking your progress toward achieving goals is essential for aligning with personal and professional growth.

- **Progress Check-Ins**: Schedule weekly or monthly check-ins to evaluate your progress toward your goals.
- **Milestones**: Break down big goals into smaller milestones. Each milestone acts as a progress marker, giving you a sense of accomplishment.
- **Reflection and Adjustment**: Reflect on your progress and adjust your goals. The timeline may need to be extended, or a new opportunity deserves prioritization.

* *Tips*

- **Short-Term Goals**: What immediate skills or tools do you need to familiarize yourself with before starting?

- **Long-Term Goals**: Where do you see your career heading in the flexible work landscape over the next 3-5 years?
- **SMART Goals**: Make sure your goals are Specific, Measurable, Achievable, Relevant, and Time-bound.

Examples of Goals:

- "Learn how to use the company's project management software within two weeks."
- "Attend one online networking event monthly to expand my professional connections."
- "Complete a certification course related to my field within six months."

2.3 NAVIGATING THE JOB MARKET FOR FLEXIBLE ROLES

Identifying Opportunities

Finding the right flexible work opportunity starts with knowing where to look.

- **Niche Job Boards**: Explore specialized job boards like FlexJobs, Remote.co, Timewise, and We Work Remotely. They curate listings for remote and flexible work positions.
- **Networking**: Leverage your existing network by reaching out to colleagues or peers working in flexible roles for potential referrals. Attend virtual meetups

and industry webinars to connect with like-minded professionals.
- **Company Websites**: Research companies that offer flexible work arrangements and monitor their career pages for openings.

Tips

- Use advanced search filters and keywords on employment websites like seek.com, indeed.com, and job boards to focus on specific work models (e.g., remote, hybrid, flexible, part-time, job sharing)
- Don't rule out job adverts that don't mention flexibility. If you are a good fit, approach the hiring person to determine if the company is open to flexible work options.
- Join LinkedIn groups that discuss flexible work to stay updated on trends and job leads.

Assessing Employer Flexibility

Understanding and confirming an employer's commitment to flexible work is crucial before accepting an offer.

- **Job Description**: Analyze the language used in job postings. Companies genuinely committed to flexibility often emphasize benefits like flexible schedules, remote work, or home office expenses.
- **Company Reviews**: Review employee experiences on platforms like Glassdoor, focusing on flexibility policies and management attitudes.

- **Interview Questions**: Ask direct questions during interviews about the company's approach to flexible work, expectations, and support mechanisms.

Key Criteria:

- Look for companies offering flexible work as part of their core policies rather than as a temporary perk.
- Seek organizations that provide digital tools, training, and support for flexible work success.

Tips

- Tailor your application to highlight your skills and readiness for flexible work.
- Resume: Emphasize previous experiences in flexible or autonomous roles.
- Include skills like time management, communication, and proficiency in using digital collaboration tools.
- Cover Letter: Express your enthusiasm for flexible work and how your background aligns with the company's work culture.
- Specify how you would address and contribute to the company's goals while working flexibly.

Interview Preparation

Communicate your ability to succeed in flexible work arrangements during your interview.

- **Discuss Experiences:** Share specific examples of projects you managed successfully in flexible environments.
- **Highlight Skills:** Emphasize your adaptability, proactiveness, and ability to work independently and in teams.
- **Ask Questions**: Inquire about the tools, support, and processes used for flexible work to show you're proactive and prepared.

**Important Note*

It is important to note that when job hunting for flexible work, not all jobs fit the flexible work model. For example, remember that not all jobs can be done remotely. Some industry sectors are more compatible with flexible work than others. For example, finance, communications and media, technology, or education generally feature more flexible jobs than agriculture and construction. Even jobs that can be performed remotely may not be so due to specific industry or company guidelines or explicit requirements for physical presence in workplaces. Use the suggested keywords and search filters around flexible work models that help narrow down your search results.

2.4 NEGOTIATING FLEXIBLE WORK ARRANGEMENTS WITH YOUR EMPLOYER

Building a Proposal

A strong proposal helps your employer see the value of flexible arrangements.

- **Benefits to the Employer**: Outline how flexibility can improve productivity, reduce costs, and enhance employee satisfaction.
- **Role Suitability**: Identify aspects of your role that lend themselves well to flexible work, like project-based tasks or roles requiring independent focus.
- **Implementation Plan**: Detail how you will maintain communication, meet deadlines, and address challenges remotely.

** Tips*

- Provide data or case studies demonstrating how flexible work can benefit similar roles or industries.
- Suggest strategies for measuring success and key performance indicators (KPIs) for ongoing evaluation.

Negotiation Techniques

Effective negotiation requires balancing both employee and employer needs.

- **Start with Mutual Benefits:** Begin by highlighting how flexible work benefits both parties and can improve productivity.
- **Be Flexible:** Show willingness to negotiate schedules, location, or role modifications.
- **Clarify Expectations:** Set clear expectations around communication, availability, and deliverables to build trust.

Trial Periods

A trial period provides a safe testing ground for flexible work.

- **Limited Duration:** Propose a short trial period (e.g., one to three months) with a clear start and end date.
- **Performance Metrics:** Define metrics for evaluating success, like meeting deadlines or maintaining productivity.
- **Feedback Mechanisms:** Establish regular check-ins for feedback and course correction.

Documenting Agreements

Having clear written agreements helps avoid future misunderstandings.

- **Terms**: Outline expectations regarding work hours, communication, and availability.
- **Tools and Support**: Specify which tools, training, or support the employer will provide.
- **Review Cycle**: Agree on a timeline for periodic reviews to adjust or renew the arrangement.

2.5 THE MENTAL SHIFT: PREPARING FOR A NEW WAY OF WORKING

Transitioning to flexible work requires a shift in mindset that embraces autonomy and self-care.

Embracing Autonomy

Flexible work often means taking the reins and being responsible for your productivity.

- **Understand Responsibility**: With autonomy comes responsibility for meeting deadlines, managing projects, and achieving goals. Shift your mindset to see these tasks as empowering rather than burdensome.
- **Self-Management Tools**: Use calendars, task managers, and productivity apps to set goals, prioritize tasks, and monitor your progress.
- **Celebrate Wins**: Recognize your achievements, whether big or small, to reward and reinforce positive behavior and maintain motivation.

** Tips*

- Set up daily and weekly routines to structure your day.
- Experiment with time-management techniques like Pomodoro or time blocking to maximize productivity.

Adapting Communication Styles

Effective communication is essential in flexible work, especially in remote teams.

- **Clarity**: Be concise and straightforward in written and verbal communication. Confirm understanding to avoid misinterpretations.
- **Frequency**: Keep communication consistent with your team to ensure alignment on goals and deliverables.
- **Channels**: Choose the appropriate channels for different purposes—email, chat, and video. Reserve video calls for complex discussions, use messaging apps, and chat for quick updates.

* *Tips*

- Schedule regular check-ins with your team to stay informed and connected.
- Be mindful of the tone you use in written communications. Tone can often be misinterpreted.

Overcoming Isolation

Flexible work can be isolating if you're used to daily in-person interactions.

- **Virtual Coworking**: Join virtual coworking sessions where people work independently but share space virtually, mimicking the office atmosphere.

- **Online Communities**: Engage in online forums, professional groups, or Slack channels to connect with like-minded professionals.
- **Regular Check-Ins**: Arrange frequent check-ins with colleagues or friends to maintain a social connection.

* Tips

- Plan outings or activities outside of work to maintain a social life.
- Consider working occasionally from a coworking space or cafe for a change of scenery.

Maintaining Work-Life Balance

One of the biggest challenges in flexible work is maintaining boundaries between professional and personal time.

- **Clear Boundaries**: Establish and stick to work hours, letting others know when you're available and when you're not.
- **Dedicated Workspace**: Separate your workspace from your personal space to maintain a mental distinction between work and relaxation.
- **Regular Breaks**: Schedule breaks throughout your day to recharge. Step outside for fresh air, stretch, or grab a coffee to clear your mind.
- **After-Hours Rituals**: Develop rituals, such as shutting down your computer, tidying up your workspace, or changing clothes to signal the end of the workday.

Tips

- Create a clear plan for your workday and prioritize tasks to avoid working overtime.
- Dedicate time to hobbies or activities that help you unwind.

CHAPTER 3
KEYS TO SUCCESS OF THE FLEXIBLE WORKER

In flexible work, success hinges on productivity, discipline, and self-motivation. Without the traditional structures of office life, you're responsible for managing your time, projects, and relationships. Here's how to build a strong foundation for thriving in this environment:

3.1 DESIGNING YOUR ULTIMATE HOME OFFICE

A well-designed home office can be the cornerstone of productivity and well-being. Creating a space that aligns with ergonomic principles and personal preferences can cultivate a work environment that keeps you focused, healthy, and motivated.

Ergonomic Principles

An ergonomic workspace is crucial to prevent strain and injury while working. **Chair and Desk:**

- Chair: Choose an adjustable chair with lumbar support that allows your feet to rest flat on the floor and your knees to be at a 90-degree angle.
- Desk: Set your desk height so your elbows rest comfortably at a 90-degree angle when typing.

Monitor Placement:

- Place your monitor about an arm's length away, positioned at eye level.
- Use a monitor stand or stack books to achieve the right height.

Accessories:

- Use an ergonomic keyboard and mouse to reduce wrist strain.
- Use a footrest if your chair height makes keeping your feet flat on the floor challenging.

* Tips

- Stand up, stretch, or walk around every hour to relieve muscle tension.
- Switch between sitting and standing with a height-adjustable desk.

Lighting and Space

Lighting and workspace organization have significant effects on productivity and mental health. **Natural Light:**

- Set up your desk near a window to take advantage of natural light, which boosts mood and reduces eye strain.
- Use sheer curtains or blinds to minimize glare.

Artificial Lighting:

- Complement natural light with a desk lamp featuring adjustable brightness to reduce eye strain during evening hours.

Workspace Organization:

- Arrange your desk to keep essential items within reach and minimize clutter.
- Use drawers, trays, or organizers to maintain a tidy workspace.

* Tips

- Avoid working directly in front of windows, which can create distracting glares.
- If possible, face your desk toward an open room or window for a more expansive and inspiring view.

Minimizing Distractions

Creating a distraction-free zone is vital to maintaining focus.
Physical Boundaries:

- Dedicate a separate room or corner as your workspace.

- Use room dividers, curtains, or noise-canceling headphones if you share the space.

Digital Distractions:

- Use browser extensions to block distracting websites.
- Mute non-essential notifications during work hours.

* Tips

- Inform family or housemates of your work hours to reduce interruptions.
- Set a timer to stay focused and take breaks at regular intervals.

Personalization for Motivation

Adding personal touches can make your workspace more motivating and enjoyable. **Decor:**

- Include photos, artwork, or plants to create a calming and uplifting atmosphere.
- Use color schemes that evoke positive emotions and concentration.

Comfort Items:

- To enhance comfort, keep a cozy blanket, ergonomic cushion, or favorite mug nearby.
- Play background music or ambient sounds that help you relax and focus.

Tips

- Arrange items that remind you of goals or successes to stay motivated.
- Rotate decor periodically to keep your workspace feeling fresh and inspiring.

3.2 TIME MANAGEMENT TECHNIQUES FOR THE FLEXIBLE WORKER

Managing time effectively is critical for productivity and work-life balance when working flexibly. Here are some essential techniques to help you navigate your day:

Prioritization Methods

Determining which tasks are most important or urgent ensures you can prioritize your time more effectively. **Eisenhower Box:**

- **Divide tasks into four categories:**

1. Urgent and Important: Tasks that need immediate attention, such as tight deadlines.
2. Important but Not Urgent: Long-term projects requiring planning and steady progress.
3. Urgent but Not Important: Delegate these tasks if possible.
4. Not Urgent and Not Important: Minimize or eliminate these distractions.

ABC Analysis:

- A: High-value tasks crucial to achieving major goals.
- B: Important tasks with a moderate impact on goals.
- C: Low-impact tasks that could be delegated or deprioritized.

Tips

- Use one of the above-suggested methods to focus on critical, high-value tasks.
- Delegate or deprioritize less important, low-impact tasks.
- Reassess priorities weekly to adapt to changing circumstances.
- Tackle the most challenging or high-priority tasks early in the day.

Pomodoro Technique

This technique involves alternating focused work periods with short breaks.

- Work Periods: Work in 25-minute intervals, focusing on a single task without distractions.
- Short Breaks: Take a 5-minute break after each 25-minute interval to rest your mind.
- Long Breaks: After four sessions (2 hours), take an extended break (15-30 minutes) to recharge.

* Tips

- Use a timer to stay on track or apps designed specifically for this technique, such as Focus Mode, Forest, or Pomodor
- Utilize breaks for light stretching, fresh air, or grabbing a healthy snack.

Batching Tasks

Grouping similar tasks helps reduce mental fatigue from frequent context-switching.

- **Identify Similar Tasks:** Examples include answering emails, making phone calls, or writing.
- **Block Time:** Dedicate a time block to each group, focusing only on that category of tasks.
- **Review and Refine:** Adjust groupings and schedules as you become more familiar with your workload.

* Tips

- Schedule focused work during peak productivity hours.
- Leave time for creative or varied tasks to avoid monotony.

Setting Boundaries

Clear work boundaries are crucial for avoiding burnout and maintaining a work-life balance.

- **Define Work Hours**: Choose specific start and end times that fit your lifestyle and stick to them. Communicate these hours to family, friends, and colleagues.
- **Create an End-of-Day Routine**: Closeout tasks, set priorities for the next day, and log off from work accounts.
- **Turn Off Notifications**: Silence notifications during non-working hours to fully disconnect.

Tips

- Schedule time for breaks, exercise, and social activities to avoid feeling isolated.
- Regularly review your routine and adjust boundaries to meet your personal needs.

3.3 THE ART OF MINIMIZING DISTRACTIONS AND PROCRASTINATION

Distractions and procrastination are productivity killers that can sneak up on anyone working flexibly. Here's how to effectively minimize their impact:

Identifying Distractions

The first step in reducing distractions is understanding what derails your focus. **Personal Distractions:**

- Mental: Intrusive thoughts about personal issues or upcoming tasks.
- Physical: Feeling tired, hungry, or restless.

Environmental Distractions:

- Home: Interruptions from family, pets, or household chores.
- Digital: Social media, emails, or non-work-related notifications.

* Tips

- Keep a log of interruptions to identify patterns and causes.
- Adjust your workspace and schedule to minimize distractions.

Use of Technology

Clever use of technology can minimize distractions and prevent procrastination.

- **Distraction-Blocking Apps**: Use browser extensions or apps like StayFocusd and Freedom to block distracting websites.
- **Task Management Tools**: Tools like Trello, Asana, or Todoist can organize tasks, set deadlines, and send reminders.
- **Time Tracking Software**: Apps like Toggl or RescueTime help monitor time spent on tasks and identify areas for improvement.

* Tips

- Set up non-essential email and social media notifications to mute during work hours.
- Establish focused work periods using a timer or Pomodoro technique apps.

Building Self-Discipline

Strengthening self-discipline is crucial for minimizing procrastination.

- **Clear Goals**: Set clear, attainable goals that motivate action rather than overwhelm. (Refer to section 2.2 *Setting Personal and Professional Goals*)
- **Reward System**: Introduce a reward system for achieving specific milestones, like a snack break or social activity.
- **Visual Reminders**: Post visual reminders, such as quotes or timelines, to reinforce goals.

* Tips

- Review goals regularly to maintain focus and stay motivated.
- Start with small, manageable tasks to build momentum.

Creating Accountability

Accountability partners or groups can keep you on track and minimize procrastination.

- **Accountability Partners:** Find a trusted colleague or friend to share goals and progress regularly.
- **Online Accountability Groups**: Join LinkedIn, Facebook, or Slack groups where members share similar goals.
- **Team Accountability**: If working within a team, set shared milestones and celebrate progress together.

Tips

- Schedule regular check-ins with your manager and colleagues to discuss progress and challenges.
- Offer positive reinforcement and constructive feedback to keep each other motivated.

3.4 ESTABLISHING A POWERFUL DAILY ROUTINE

Creating a powerful daily routine is crucial for productivity and mental well-being. Establishing purposeful morning and evening habits and scheduling adequate breaks while maintaining a balanced lifestyle can help you achieve more.

Importance of Routine

A structured routine provides the stability needed to stay organized and productive.

- **Predictability**: A set routine allows you to anticipate and prepare for the day's challenges.
- **Decision Fatigue**: Fewer daily decisions mean more mental energy for creative problem-solving.

- **Consistency**: Consistent habits reinforce productivity and foster a sense of accomplishment.

Tips

- Start small and build habits gradually to establish long-term changes.
- Incorporate enjoyable activities to create a positive association with your routine.

Morning Routines

A productive morning routine sets the tone for a successful day.

- **Physical Activity**: Light exercise or stretching helps boost energy and concentration.
- **Mindfulness**: Meditation or deep breathing exercises reduce stress and enhance focus.
- **Healthy Breakfast**: A balanced breakfast with protein and complex carbohydrates fuels your body.
- **Daily Goals**: Review your to-do list and prioritize tasks to clarify your goals.

Tips

- Create a consistent wake-up time to regulate your internal clock.
- Limit exposure to social media or email to avoid unnecessary stress.

Breaks and Downtime

Breaks are essential to maintain productivity and prevent burnout. **Short Breaks**:

- If you are using the Pomodoro technique (Refer to section *3.2 Time Management Techniques for the Flexible Worker*), take a 5-minute break after each 25-minute interval. Otherwise, take a 5-to-10-minute break every hour to stretch, hydrate, or walk.

Long Breaks:

- Incorporate a longer break (15-30 minutes) after intense focus periods or after four sessions using the Pomodoro technique.

Unplugging:

- Disconnect from work during breaks to give your mind time to recharge.

* Tips

- Plan by scheduling breaks into your calendar as you would work meetings. This means blocking out time for work and rest breaks.
- Use breaks for activities that promote relaxation, like reading or listening to music.
- Be consistent when scheduling your work and rest breaks. Incorporate the Pomodoro Technique (section 3.2) into your daily routine.

Evening Wind-Down

An evening routine helps separate work from personal time and prepares you for restful sleep.

- **End-of-Day Review**: Review your progress, identify challenges, and outline tasks for the next day.
- **Physical Activity**: Light exercise, yoga, or stretching can relieve tension built up during the day.
- **Unwinding Activities**: Enjoy relaxing activities like reading, crafting, or listening to music.
- **Sleep Preparation**: Reduce screen time and keep a consistent bedtime to improve sleep quality.

* Tips

- Avoid heavy meals and caffeine before bed to promote better sleep.
- Practice gratitude by noting daily achievements or positive moments.

3.5 THE ROLE OF PHYSICAL FITNESS IN ENHANCING PRODUCTIVITY

Physical fitness significantly enhances productivity, especially when working in a flexible environment where maintaining energy and focus is crucial.

Exercise and Mental Clarity

Regular physical activity directly impacts mental clarity, focus, and cognitive performance.

- **Stress Reduction**: Exercise lowers cortisol levels, reducing stress and anxiety while improving mood.
- **Increased Blood Flow**: Physical activity increases blood flow to the brain, enhancing concentration and decision-making.
- **Neurotransmitter Release**: Workouts stimulate endorphins, dopamine, and serotonin, boosting creativity and motivation.

Tips

- Aim for at least 30-minutes of moderate exercise daily, such as brisk walking or cycling.
- Choose activities that you enjoy to increase consistency.

Incorporating Movement into the Workday

Short exercise breaks and ergonomic adjustments can help you stay active even during the busiest days.

- **Short Exercise Breaks**: Set a timer to remind you to take a break according to your work-rest schedule. Do light stretching, walking, or yoga.
- **Standing Desks**: Alternate between sitting and standing using height-adjustable desks or desk risers.
- **Walk-and-Talk Meetings**: Take phone calls or participate in brainstorming sessions while walking.

* Tips

- Incorporate stretches or quick workouts like jumping jacks or skipping during breaks.
- Arrange your workspace for extra space and easy access to workout equipment or a yoga mat.

Fitness Routines for Remote Workers

A tailored fitness routine ensures you maintain your health goals within a flexible schedule.

- **Short Workouts**: High-intensity interval training (HIIT) and circuit workouts can be effective in 15-20 minutes.
- **Home Workout Plans**: Follow online fitness classes or use apps offering guided workouts at home.
- **Scheduled Exercise Blocks**: Block out specific times in your calendar for workouts like any other work commitment. Follow your work-rest schedule.

* Tips

- Keep a log or use fitness trackers to monitor your progress.
- Mix up routines to include walking, yoga, dancing, or bodyweight exercises.

Impact on Energy Levels

Consistent physical activity leads to sustainable energy levels throughout the day.

- **Improved Endurance**: Strength and cardio exercises improve stamina, helping you stay energized longer.
- **Reduced Fatigue**: Physical activity encourages better sleep patterns, reducing daytime fatigue.
- **Balanced Nutrition**: Exercise increases the appetite for healthier food choices that sustain energy.

* Tips

- Avoid exercising at night close to bedtime to prevent sleep disruption.
- Pair workouts with a nutritious diet to optimize energy levels.

CHAPTER 4
MASTERING THE TOOLS OF THE TRADE

Flexible work relies heavily on the right tools and practices to remain productive, connected, and secure. This chapter will guide you through the essential technologies needed for flexible work and strategies to build relationships and ensure data security in remote environments.

4.1 COMMUNICATION TOOLS: BEYOND EMAIL AND ZOOM

In a world where digital communication is the backbone of flexible work, relying solely on traditional tools like email and Zoom can be limiting. Let's explore alternative tools that cater to diverse communication needs, how to choose the right ones, and ways to optimize them for maximum productivity.

Exploring Available Tools

Different tasks require different tools. Here's a rundown of alternatives for specific communication purposes:

- **Instant Messaging**: For real-time conversations, tools like Slack, Microsoft Teams, and Discord provide quick access to colleagues. They support file sharing, topic-based channels, and integrations with other apps.
- **Video Conferencing**: Zoom and Google Meet are tools widely used for video meetings. However, alternatives like Microsoft Teams and Cisco Webex offer collaborative features such as shared whiteboards and live captions.
- **Asynchronous Communication**: Loom and Vidyard allow you to record and share short videos for asynchronous feedback, helping to reduce unnecessary meetings.
- **Project Management**: Tools like Asana, Monday.com, and Trello make project progress visible to all team members and incorporate messaging features.

* Tips

- Select messaging apps based on team size, security requirements, and communication frequency.
- Choose video conferencing tools that align with the team's meeting style and technical preferences.
- Try before you buy by opting in for free trial periods where available.

Choosing the Right Tools

Selecting the most suitable tools depends on both individual and team requirements:

- **Purpose and Functionality**: Identify the core purpose (e.g., brainstorming, daily updates, file sharing) and ensure the tool offers specific features like screen sharing, threaded conversations, or advanced search.
- **Team Dynamics**: Assess your team members' communication preferences and skill levels. Some tools are intuitive, while others have a steeper learning curve.
- **Security and Compliance**: Check for encryption, data privacy policies, and compliance standards, especially for sensitive or confidential information.
- **Integration**: Consider tools that integrate with existing software to streamline workflows.

Tips

- Pilot new tools with a small group before implementing them team-wide.
- Provide training sessions to help team members become familiar with the new tools.

Integration for Efficiency

Integrating communication tools with other apps can improve workflows and productivity:

- **Project Management Integration**: Connect messaging apps like Slack or Teams with project management software to receive notifications directly within chat channels.

- **Calendar Integration**: Sync video conferencing tools with calendars to schedule and join meetings effortlessly.
- **Cloud Storage Integration**: Link file-sharing tools like Dropbox or Google Drive with messaging platforms for direct access to shared files.

* Tips

- Use workflow automation tools like Zapier to automate routine tasks between apps.
- Regularly audit tool usage to identify redundant or underutilized apps.

Customization and Settings

Tailoring your communication tools can make them more efficient and suited to your work habits:

- **Notification Settings**: Adjust notifications based on urgency or priority to minimize distractions while staying informed.
- **Workspaces and Channels**: Create dedicated channels or workspaces for specific teams, projects, or interests to organize discussions.
- **Shortcut Keys**: Learn keyboard shortcuts to navigate faster through tasks like switching channels, muting/unmuting, or searching.

Tips

- Set status messages to inform colleagues when you're in focus mode or available.
- Create message templates for frequently used responses to save time.

4.2 ACHIEVING CLARITY IN VIRTUAL COMMUNICATIONS

Clear communication is crucial in any work setting, but it's essential in flexible work arrangements where most interactions happen virtually. Here's how to achieve clarity in your writing, video meetings, feedback loops, and when working with global teams.

Writing Skills

Effective writing can make a significant difference in virtual communication.

- **Clear and Concise:** Aim for brevity. Focus on the main message and avoid unnecessary jargon. Structure emails or messages using short paragraphs and bullet points.
- **Action-Oriented**: Make your requests or actions explicit. Use phrases like "Please review by Friday" or "Action required: update the project plan."
- **Tone and Context**: Be mindful of the tone used in your writing. What you intend as light-hearted can come across differently in writing, so clarify with emoticons or include a disclaimer if needed.

Tips

- Re-read messages before sending them to catch ambiguities or errors.
- Use subject lines that summarize the main message.

Video Conference Etiquette

Video conferencing is integral to virtual teamwork, and good etiquette ensures productive and professional meetings.

- **Pre-Meeting Preparation**: Share agendas in advance and encourage participants to familiarize themselves with the discussion points.
- **Camera and Background**: Use a clean, clutter-free background and good lighting. Position the camera at eye level and dress professionally.
- **Mute When Necessary**: Mute your microphone to avoid unintended background noise whenever you're not speaking. If noise suppression filters are available, turn them on.
- **Stay Engaged**: Nod, smile, or use gestures to acknowledge speakers. Avoid multitasking or distractions when on video.

Tips

- Record meetings when appropriate to accommodate those who can't attend.
- Set up norms around speaking turns, use of the chat, or raising hands.

Feedback Loops

Regular feedback is key to maintaining alignment in flexible teams.

- **Frequent Check-Ins**: Schedule weekly or biweekly check-ins with team members to discuss progress, challenges, and expectations.
- **Constructive Feedback**: Frame feedback positively. Instead of "You didn't finish this task," try "Let's work together on prioritizing this task."
- **Recognition**: Recognize and celebrate achievements to build morale and reinforce positive behavior.

** Tips*

- Encourage two-way feedback to understand each team member's needs.
- Document feedback sessions to track progress.

Cultural Sensitivity

Global teams often come from diverse backgrounds. Understanding cultural nuances can prevent misunderstandings.

- **Language Barriers**: Be patient with colleagues for whom English isn't the first language. Avoid idioms or region-specific expressions.
- **Cultural Norms**: Research common communication styles, holidays, social norms, and work practices in different cultures to show respect and understanding.

- **Time Zones:** Schedule meetings at convenient times for all participants and offer asynchronous communication options.

Tips

- Encourage team members to share their preferences and cultural nuances.
- Rotate meeting times to accommodate different time zones.

4.3 STAYING CONNECTED: BUILDING RELATIONSHIPS IN A REMOTE WORLD

World Staying connected is vital for personal and professional alignment in remote work environments. Regular check-ins and virtual team events not only foster camaraderie but also reduce feelings of isolation, making each team member feel connected and engaged. Here's how these activities, along with mentorship, networking, and adding personal touches, can help build strong relationships:

Check-ins

Regular check-ins with team members help maintain alignment and build a supportive work environment.

- **One-on-One Meetings**: Schedule regular one-on-one meetings with direct reports to discuss goals, challenges, and development. This will give each team member personalized support and guidance.

- **Team Stand-Ups**: Daily or weekly stand-up meetings enable the team to share updates, identify blockers, and synchronize efforts.
- **Pulse Surveys**: Conduct short pulse surveys to gauge team morale and get actionable feedback on how the team feels.

Tips

- Keep meetings brief but focused. Encourage open communication and practice active listening.
- Mix video and audio calls based on participants' preferences and bandwidth.

Virtual Team Events

Virtual team-building activities foster camaraderie and team spirit, reducing feelings of isolation.

- **Game Sessions**: Host online game sessions like trivia or Pictionary for fun and casual team interaction.
- **Skill Sharing**: Organize knowledge-sharing sessions where team members teach a hobby, craft, or technical skill.
- **Virtual Coffee Breaks**: Schedule informal virtual coffee breaks or lunch hours where people can chat casually.

Tips

- Allow flexible timing so team members can attend at their convenience.

- Consider occasional in-person meetups if teams are geographically close.

Mentoring and Networking

Building a remote network can be challenging but rewarding with the right strategies.

- **Mentorship Programs**: Establish a mentorship program within the company to connect experienced employees with newcomers.
- **Professional Organization**s: Encourage joining professional organizations and attending virtual conferences to expand One's network.
- **Alum Networks**: Tap into alum networks from previous workplaces or educational institutions to find mentoring or networking opportunities.

** Tips*

- Schedule virtual coffee chats with new connections to nurture relationships.
- Develop personal learning plans with your mentor to track progress.

Personal Touches

Adding personal touches to your communication helps build rapport and strengthens relationships.

- **Celebrate Milestones**: Recognize birthdays, work anniversaries, or significant personal

milestones with team-wide messages or small virtual gifts.
- **Check-In Beyond Work**: Ask about family or hobbies, and listen actively when team members share personal stories.
- **Handwritten Notes**: Send handwritten notes or small tokens of appreciation for exceptional achievements or support during challenging times.

Tips

- Create a digital birthday or anniversary calendar for team members.
- Incorporate humor and casual conversations to lighten up interactions.

4.4 PROTECTING YOUR DATA: CYBERSECURITY FOR THE HOME WORKER

Maintaining robust cybersecurity practices is essential when working remotely. Follow these strategies to secure data and devices, leverage VPNs, avoid phishing and scams, and ensure regular data backups.

Best Practices for Security

Maintaining strong security practices protects sensitive data and ensures safe connectivity.

- **Regular Software Updates**: Enable automatic updates for your operating system, antivirus software,

and other applications. Updated software often addresses newly detected security vulnerabilities.
- **Strong Passwords**: Use unique, strong passwords that combine letters, numbers, and symbols. Avoid reusing passwords across different platforms.
- **Two-Factor Authentication**: Enable two-factor authentication (2FA) wherever possible for an extra layer of security.

Tips

- Consider using a password manager to generate, store, and retrieve unique passwords.
- Review privacy settings for applications and turn off unnecessary data sharing.

VPN Use

Using Virtual Private Networks (VPNs) is crucial for secure online activity.

- **Encrypted Connections**: VPNs encrypt internet traffic, protecting sensitive data from interception, especially when using public Wi-Fi.
- **Remote Access**: Provide secure access to company networks to ensure data is protected when accessed from outside the office.

Tips

- Choose a reliable VPN provider that doesn't log user activity.

- Test your VPN connection regularly to ensure consistent protection is in place.

Phishing and Scams

Phishing attacks target remote workers, making recognizing and avoiding them essential.

- **Suspicious Emails**: Avoid unsolicited emails or messages asking for personal information or containing unexpected links.
- **Verify Sources**: Confirm with the sender before sharing sensitive data if an email seems suspicious.
- **Urgent Requests**: Be wary of urgent requests, such as immediate payment or password reset, as these are common phishing tactics.

** Tips*

- Report suspicious emails to your IT department or email provider.
- Avoid downloading attachments or clicking links in unverified emails.
- Treat all emails from senders you don't recognize as suspicious.

Data Backup

Regular data backups ensure essential information is not lost in case of a security breach.

- **Automated Backups**: Schedule automatic backups of important files and data to secure external drives or cloud storage.
- **Redundant Storage**: Use multiple storage locations to minimize data loss risks. Consider using both cloud and physical storage.
- **Testing and Encryption**: Periodically test backup files to ensure they work correctly and encrypt sensitive data for added security.

* Tips

- Keep backup devices disconnected from the primary system to prevent ransomware from spreading.
- Label and organize backup files for quick retrieval.

Incorporating these practices into your remote work routine can significantly improve cybersecurity and protect sensitive information.

CHAPTER 5
BUILDING AND MANAGING REMOTE TEAMS

In this new world of flexible work and in particular, remote work, the ability to build and manage effective remote teams has become a critical skill for leaders. Successfully leading a dispersed team requires a unique approach to communication, collaboration, and team cohesion. This chapter delves into the essential strategies for creating a strong remote team, from establishing trust and fostering a positive team culture to leveraging technology for seamless collaboration.

5.1 THE FOUNDATIONS OF TRUST IN REMOTE TEAMS

Trust is the bedrock of any successful team, and it's especially crucial in remote work, where face-to-face interactions are limited. Trust ensures seamless collaboration and high morale. Building this trust requires consistent practices around transparency, communication, empowerment, and shared achievements.

Building Trust

Establishing trust in remote teams starts with intentional leadership and genuine connection. **Transparency:**

- Leaders should be open about company goals, challenges, and decisions, creating a culture where no question is off-limits.
- Encourage honest conversations and ensure all team members feel comfortable sharing concerns.

Reliability: Consistently deliver on promises and deadlines. If delays arise, communicate early and often.

* Tips

- Create a virtual "open door" policy for questions or suggestions.
- Foster a non-judgmental space for mistakes or missteps.

Communication Transparency

Open, honest communication keeps remote teams aligned and strengthens trust. **Clear Channels:**

- Establish dedicated channels for different types of communication, such as project updates or personal check-ins. Set brief 10-15 minute daily check-ins.

Feedback Culture:

- Encourage a culture of regular feedback, where constructive criticism is valued, and personal growth is prioritized. Create a safe environment for team members to give honest, open feedback. Make this the norm, not just during performance reviews.

Knowledge Sharing:

- Implement a system where knowledge and resources are readily accessible to all team members by setting up a knowledge base.

* Tips

- Regularly update the team on project progress and critical decisions.
- Rotate meeting facilitators to give each team member a chance to lead.
- Share collective knowledge with all team members with a knowledge base.

Empowerment and Autonomy

Empowering team members with autonomy boosts their confidence and reinforces trust. **Clear Expectations:**

- Set clear goals and expectations, then give team members the freedom to approach their work in their own way. These can be short-term daily and weekly goals, i.e., what outcomes they must achieve today or this week. Then, set medium- to long-term goals that are reflected in their scheduled performance reviews.

Ownership:

- Encourage ownership of projects, allowing team members to take responsibility for successes and failures.

Decision-Making:

- Involve team members in critical decisions affecting their work, reinforcing that their input is valued.

* Tips

- Assign stretch projects that challenge team members to grow.
- Recognize innovative approaches and celebrate creativity.

Measuring and Sharing Success

Tracking progress and sharing achievements keeps the team motivated and aligned. **Measuring Success:**

- Set up metrics that reflect individual and team contributions, such as project milestones, customer satisfaction scores, or innovative solutions.

Sharing Wins:

- Celebrate team successes in meetings or through internal newsletters. Highlight how everyone's efforts contributed to the outcome.

Feedback on Success:

- Collect feedback on recent achievements to identify strengths and areas for improvement.

* Tips

- Create a "Wall of Wins" where team members can publicly share their achievements.
- Celebrating small wins along the way creates confidence and motivation for future bigger wins.
- Reflect on projects post-completion to recognize efforts and analyze lessons learned.

5.2 VIRTUAL TEAM-BUILDING ACTIVITIES THAT WORK

Effective team-building activities can transform a group of distant individuals into a unified team that collaborates seamlessly. Here's how to plan and implement virtual activities that foster team spirit.

Effective Activities

Not all team-building activities resonate equally with everyone, so choosing ones that appeal to varied interests and goals is crucial. Here are a few proven ideas: **Virtual Escape Rooms**:

- Challenge team members to solve puzzles and riddles together. The teamwork required can build communication and problem-solving skills.

Trivia Quizzes:

- Host quizzes on general knowledge, niche topics, or team-specific facts. It's a light-hearted way to bond over shared interests.

Show and Tell:

- Encourage members to share something meaningful, such as a hobby, recipe, or book. This personal sharing can help team members get to know each other and build empathy and understanding.

Collaborative Workshops:

- Bring the team together to learn new skills, such as using technology more effectively, writing, coding, or time-saving shortcuts. These shared learning experiences enhance camaraderie.

* Tips

Mix up different formats of activities to cater to various personalities and preferences.

Frequency and Timing

Team-building activities must occur regularly but not so often that they feel obligatory.

- **Frequency**: Monthly activities strike a good balance. More frequent events like weekly games can work for highly engaged teams.
- **Timing**: Consider everyone's time zones when scheduling.
- Align the event timing with existing meetings to minimize disruption.
- **Length**: Keep activities to 30–60 minutes to prevent fatigue and keep engagement high.

** Tips*

Include team members in planning to find a schedule that works best for everyone.

Inclusivity in Activities

Virtual activities should be accessible to all, regardless of team members' backgrounds, abilities, or interests.

- **Accessible Tech:** Use tools that are user-friendly and compatible with different devices
- **Flexible Participation:** Make activities low-pressure so members can participate comfortably.
- **Cultural Sensitivity:** Be sensitive to cultural differences and plan activities that don't alienate any team member.

- **Accommodation:** Ensure activities accommodate those with disabilities or different learning styles.

* Tips

Survey team members beforehand to understand their preferences and ensure everyone can contribute ideas.

Feedback

Feedback is critical to refining and improving team-building activities over time.

- **Anonymous Surveys**: Use anonymous surveys to capture honest opinions and team suggestions.
- **Iterative Improvements**: Be open to experimenting and iterating based on feedback to make activities more engaging and inclusive.
- **Celebrate Changes**: When changes based on team feedback are introduced, acknowledge and celebrate with the team.

* Tips

Rotate event facilitators to bring fresh ideas and perspectives to each activity.

5.3 MANAGING CROSS-CULTURAL REMOTE TEAMS

With globalization and remote work intertwined, managing

culturally diverse teams requires nuanced strategies to bridge differences and harness varied strengths.

Cultural Awareness

Cultural awareness forms the foundation for managing diverse teams effectively.

- **Education:** Take time to learn about your team's various cultural backgrounds. Understand the unique customs, communication norms, and societal values that shape their behavior.
- **Sensitivity:** Be sensitive to different cultural holidays and observances. Avoid making assumptions or generalizations based on stereotypes.
- **Resources**: Provide resources and training to help team members understand and respect each other's cultural norms.

** Tips*

Encourage open conversations about culture and identity, allowing team members to share their personal experiences.

Communication Styles

Different cultures often have varying communication preferences and expectations. **Direct vs. Indirect:**

- Some cultures prefer direct communication, while others favor subtle or indirect approaches.

- Learn these preferences and adapt your style accordingly.

Nonverbal Cues:

- Understand the nonverbal cues like gestures or facial expressions that vary across cultures.

Language Barriers:

- Simplify language when communicating with non-native speakers.
- Encourage the use of plain language in emails and messages for clarity.

* Tips

Ask clarifying questions to confirm understanding and avoid miscommunication.

Inclusive Decision-Making

Decision-making should involve input from all team members while respecting cultural nuances. **Consensus Building:**

- Some cultures value consensus, while others may be more hierarchical in decision-making.
- Balance both styles by seeking input from everyone before making key decisions.
- Incorporate Perspectives: Invite diverse perspectives, especially from those less inclined to speak up due to cultural norms.

Respect Timing:

- Give team members enough time to process and respond to decisions, especially if English isn't their first language.

* Tips

Regularly rotate decision-making roles to ensure everyone's voice is considered and respected.

Celebrating Diversity

Recognizing and celebrating cultural diversity can strengthen team cohesion and build mutual respect.

- **Virtual Celebrations:** Host virtual celebrations around cultural holidays or festivals. Allow team members to share their traditions.
- **Diversity Training:** Conduct diversity training sessions to improve awareness and acceptance.
- **Cultural Exchange**: Organize a cultural exchange where team members share unique aspects of their culture.

* Tips

Create a cultural calendar highlighting important holidays or events for team members from different countries or regions.

5.4. THE REMOTE LEADER: STRATEGIES FOR INSPIRING YOUR TEAM

Remote leadership demands a unique set of strategies to inspire, motivate, and cultivate a cohesive team from a distance. Here's how to lead effectively in a virtual landscape.

Leadership Qualities

Successful remote leaders exhibit these critical qualities:

- **Adaptability**: Navigate changing conditions and tech challenges smoothly, modeling flexibility for the team.
- **Empathy:** Demonstrate empathy by actively listening to team members and understanding their unique needs.
- **Proactivity**: Anticipate potential issues before they arise and communicate solutions.
- **Clarity**: Set clear goals and expectations, ensuring every team member understands their role.

* *Tips*

Balance these qualities with humility, acknowledging your limitations, and encouraging team feedback.

Motivation Techniques

Keeping a remote team motivated requires thoughtful and consistent effort. **Recognition:**

- Recognize individual and team achievements publicly.
- Personalized appreciation (emails, small gifts, etc.) can reinforce positive behavior.

Goal Setting:

- Set team and individual goals that align with the overall company vision.
- Break down significant objectives into manageable milestones to build momentum.

Incentives:

- Offer meaningful incentives like extra time off, skill development courses, or performance bonuses.

* Tips

Match motivational techniques to individual preferences to enhance their impact.

Professional Development

Support your team's growth with opportunities for continuous learning and skill enhancement.

- **Skill Building**: Encourage team members to explore courses, certifications, or webinars that align with their career goals.
- **Mentorship**: Pair less-experienced employees with mentors for guidance and support.

- **Career Pathing**: Help team members outline a clear career path within the company and identify skills needed to progress.

Tips

Investing in team development will foster loyalty and long-term engagement.

Conflict Resolution

Conflicts in remote teams can quickly escalate due to communication challenges, so a proactive approach is crucial.

- **Clear Policies**: Establish clear guidelines on acceptable behavior and reporting conflicts.
- **Mediation**: Act as a dispute mediator to understand each party's perspective and seek mutually beneficial solutions.
- **Timely Response**: Address conflicts promptly to prevent festering issues from undermining morale.
- **Restorative Approach**: Encourage a restorative approach where parties work together to rebuild trust and collaboration.

Tips

Create anonymous feedback channels where team members can express concerns freely.

5.5 PERFORMANCE MEASUREMENT AND FEEDBACK IN A FLEXIBLE TEAM

Ensuring your team stays aligned with organizational goals requires clear expectations, fair measurement, and regular feedback. Here's how to optimize performance management in a flexible work setting.

Setting Clear Expectations

Establishing expectations that everyone understands is vital for accountability and productivity. **Role Clarity**:

- Define each team member's role clearly, highlighting their responsibilities and how their work contributes to the broader objectives.

KPIs and Goals:

- Develop Key Performance Indicators (KPIs) that align with the team's goals.
- Involve team members in setting personal and professional goals to foster ownership.

Written Documentation:

- Write performance expectations and share them with the team.

* Tips

Review expectations periodically to adapt to evolving roles and project demands.

Performance Metrics

Developing relevant and fair performance metrics requires a careful balancing act.

- **Align with Objectives**: Ensure metrics are tied to team and company objectives, linking individual contributions and organizational success.
- **Avoid Micromanagement**: Focus on output rather than micromanaging activities or hours worked.
- **Transparency**: Be transparent about the evaluation criteria and how data is collected to avoid misunderstanding or mistrust.
- **Adjust Metrics**: Be open to adjusting metrics as necessary, considering shifts in workload, resources, or strategic priorities.

*Tips

Consider using a mix of quantitative and qualitative data to assess performance more holistically.

Regular Feedback

Providing regular and consistent feedback helps team members understand their strengths and areas for improvement. **Timely and Constructive:**

- Provide feedback promptly after key projects or milestones.
- Frame it constructively by acknowledging

achievements and offering specific suggestions for improvement.

Two-Way Conversations: Give feedback in a two-way conversation where team members can share their perspectives and ask clarifying questions.

Growth-Oriented: Focus on growth and future goals rather than dwelling on past mistakes.

* Tips

Encourage team members to request feedback to cultivate a continuous improvement culture proactively.

Adapting Feedback Methods

Feedback methods should be tailored to the virtual context, ensuring clarity and understanding.

- **Video Calls**: Schedule video calls for detailed discussions where body language can aid comprehension.
- **Written Feedback**: Summarize key points in writing after feedback sessions to reinforce understanding and provide a reference.
- **Cultural Sensitivity**: Be culturally sensitive when delivering feedback to ensure it is well-received and understood.

Tips

Use anonymous surveys occasionally to gather candid feedback from team members.

Managing a remote team can be incredibly rewarding when done right. You can build a high-performing team that thrives across distance and time zones by prioritizing trust, empathy, and clear communication.

WELCOME TO THE CLUB!

"Remember there's no such thing as a small act of kindness. Every act creates a ripple with no logical end"

SCOTT ADAMS, CREATOR OF DILBERT COMIC STRIP

Would you help someone you've never met, even if you never got credit for it?

Our mission is to make *Flex Appeal* accessible to everyone. And the only way to accomplish that mission is by reaching out to everyone.

This is where you come in. Most people judge a book by its cover (and its reviews). So here's my request on behalf of a struggling remote worker you've never met:

Please help that person by leaving this book a review.

Your review could help…

…a small business provide for their community.
…an entrepreneur support their family.
…an employee get meaningful work.
…a client transform their life.
…a dream come true.

To help, just leave a review. It takes less than 60 seconds. Simply scan the QR code below to leave your review:

If you feel good about helping a stranger, you are my kind of person. Welcome to the club. You're one of us. I'm excited to help you find happiness and success in your professional life. You'll love the strategies and tips in the coming chapters.

Thank you from the bottom of my heart.

Your biggest fan,

Desmond Winters

PS - Fun fact: If you provide something of value to another person, it makes you more valuable to them. If you believe this book will help them, send it their way.

CHAPTER 6
THE PERSONAL CHALLENGES OF FLEXIBLE WORK

In the ever-evolving landscape of flexible work, individuals often face personal challenges impacting productivity, mental health, and career growth. Let's explore these challenges and provide strategies to tackle them head-on.

6.1 HANDLING FEELINGS OF ISOLATION AND LONELINESS

Remote workers frequently report feelings of isolation, loneliness, and disconnectedness. The lack of casual social interactions in an office can lead to a sense of exclusion. These factors all lead to a negative impact on your mental health. Prolonged isolation can contribute to stress, anxiety, and decreased productivity. It is essential that you protect your emotional well-being which is crucial for maintaining motivation and satisfaction. Here are some strategies you can use to help battle these negative feelings.

* Tips

Acknowledge your emotions and seek support from trusted friends, family, or colleagues.

Creating Virtual Connections

Intentional Communication:

- Schedule regular video calls, even if it's just for informal chats.
- Be proactive in contacting coworkers for casual conversations or virtual coffee breaks.

Team Building Activities:

- Engage in virtual team-building exercises like trivia games or book clubs to foster camaraderie.

* Tips

Start team meetings with a personal check-in to strengthen the human connection.

Leveraging Online Communities

Professional Networks:

- Participate in professional networks on platforms like LinkedIn or specialized forums.
- Discuss challenges and successes with peers in similar roles.

THE PERSONAL CHALLENGES OF FLEXIBLE WORK

Support Groups:

- Join online groups focusing on remote work, productivity hacks, or mental health.
- Sharing experiences can help normalize challenges and reduce the sense of isolation.

* Tips

Be an active contributor in these communities to build meaningful connections and support.

Seeking External Activities

Hobbies and Interests:

- Pursue hobbies like fitness classes, painting, or cooking to relax and recharge.
- Attend local events or meetups to interact with people outside your immediate circle.

Volunteering:

- Volunteer in your community to meet new people and find fulfillment through giving back.

* Tips

Use time management skills to schedule non-work activities that bring you joy and fulfillment.

6.2 DRAWING BOUNDARIES: WORK-LIFE BALANCE IN PRACTICE

Importance of Physical Boundaries

In section 3.1, *Designing your Ultimate Home Office*, we discussed the importance of having clear physical boundaries to minimize distractions in your flexible workplace. Without distinct lines between professional responsibilities and personal time, work can easily creep into every aspect of your life, leading to increased stress and eventual burnout. But by setting and respecting these boundaries, you create a structured routine that allows you to fully engage in your work during designated hours and enjoy your life outside of them.

Dedicated Workspace:

- Designate a specific area at home solely for work, even if it's a small corner.
- This helps signal the start and end of the workday, reinforcing a separation between work and personal time.

Visual Cues:

- Use visual cues like a closed door or a "Do Not Disturb" sign to indicate when you're in work mode.

* Tips

Avoid working in personal spaces like the bedroom or dining table to maintain mental separation.

Setting Time Boundaries

Clear Work Hours:

- Establish specific work hours and adhere to them consistently.
- Share your schedule with family or roommates so they know when not to interrupt.

Communicating with Team Members:

- Make your availability clear to colleagues and politely enforce your boundaries.

Tips

Utilize calendar blocking to visually map out work and non-work hours. (Refer to section 3.2, *Time Management for Flexible Workers*)

Managing Expectations

Professional Expectations:

- Set realistic expectations for productivity and communicate these with your team.
- Clearly outline your availability to set limits on after-hours communication.

Personal Expectations:

- Be realistic about what can be accomplished outside work hours and share household responsibilities when possible.

* Tips

Learn to say "no" or delegate tasks that overburden your schedule.

Mindful Breaks and Downtime

- **Regular Breaks**: Integrate short, regular breaks throughout the day to step away from screens and stretch. (Refer to the *Pomodoro technique* in section 3.2).
- **Unplugging**: Unplug from work devices entirely during evenings and weekends.
- **Downtime Activities**: Schedule time for hobbies, exercise, or meditation to rejuvenate yourself.

* Tips

Set alarms or reminders to signal when it's time to take breaks and wind down.

6.3 DEALING WITH OVERWORK AND BURNOUT

In today's fast-paced work environment, especially within flexible work arrangements, the lines between professional and personal life can easily blur, leading to overwork and burnout. Recognizing and addressing these issues is crucial for maintaining productivity and overall well-being. This section explores practical strategies for identifying early signs of burnout, implementing effective prevention techniques, and creating a sustainable work routine that promotes long-term success and health. Proactively managing overwork and burnout can ensure a balanced and fulfilling work-life experience.

Recognizing the Signs

- **Physical Symptoms**: Frequent headaches, fatigue, or muscle tension could indicate that you're overextending yourself.
- **Emotional Symptoms**: Irritability, cynicism, and feeling overwhelmed may point to burnout.
- **Behavioral Changes**: Noticeable shifts, such as reduced productivity, withdrawal from responsibilities, or trouble concentrating, are early red flags.

* *Tips*

Keep a journal of your energy levels and mood patterns to help spot concerning trends.

Strategies for Prevention

- **Time Management**: Use techniques like the Pomodoro method to structure focused work periods with frequent breaks.

- **Delegation**: Don't hesitate to delegate tasks where appropriate or share responsibilities with colleagues.
- **Prioritization Techniques**: Apply prioritization frameworks like the Eisenhower Matrix (*Refer to section 3.2 Time Management Techniques for the Flexible Worker*) to distinguish between urgent and important tasks.

* Tips

Adopt a "good enough" mindset for tasks that don't require perfection.

Recovery Methods

- **Time Off**: Take mental health days or longer breaks to fully disconnect from work.
- **Professional Help**: Seek support from a therapist, counselor, or trusted coach.
- **Reassessing Workload**: Reevaluate your current workload, prioritize essential tasks, and negotiate adjustments if required.

* Tips

Combine time off with rejuvenating activities like hiking, painting, or reading for a mental reset.

Creating a Sustainable Work Routine

- **Work Hours**: Set realistic daily work hours that allow for breaks and personal time.

- **Breaks and Downtime**: Schedule brief, restorative breaks and regular downtime to recharge.
- **Long-Term Planning**: Create a flexible plan that factors in realistic workloads and leaves room for personal projects.

* Tips

Include various activities in your downtime to keep it refreshing and not routine.

6.4 OVERCOMING TECHNOLOGICAL OVERWHELM

In the era of digital transformation, technology is both a boon and a challenge. While it facilitates remote work and enhances productivity, the constant influx of tools and platforms can lead to technology overwhelm. Navigating this digital overload requires a strategic approach to streamline your tech stack, prioritize essential tools, and implement practices that promote digital well-being. This section offers practical advice on managing technology effectively, reducing screen time, and creating a balanced digital environment to ensure you remain focused, efficient, and stress-free in your flexible work setup.

Simplifying Your Tech Stack

Evaluate Your Tools: Review your current software and platforms. Which are essential, and which can be consolidated or eliminated?

- **Prioritize**: Focus on tools that are directly linked to your most critical tasks.
- **Integration Matters**: Choose tools that integrate seamlessly with your existing workflow to minimize the need for multiple logins or redundant data entry.

* Tips

To reduce tool fatigue, use a single project management tool that centralizes communication, task tracking, and file sharing.

Staying Updated Without Stress

- **Continuous Learning Plans**: Dedicate a few hours each month to upskilling on the most relevant technologies affecting your industry.
- **Trusted Sources**: Subscribe to trusted newsletters or follow tech leaders who curate valuable insights on updates.
- *Set Learning Goals*: Identify key skills or tools that will directly benefit your work and create achievable goals around them.

* Tips

Experiment with tech in a sandbox environment or free trials to learn without impacting your current projects.

Tech-Free Times

- **Scheduled Disconnects**: Schedule short breaks throughout the day and a longer tech-free period at least once a week.
- **Mindful Activities**: Engage in tech-free activities like nature walks, cooking, or reading to reset your mind.
- **No-Device Zones**: Create no-device zones in your home where you can unwind without digital distractions.

** Tips*

Try digital detox challenges by gradually increasing the hours or days of tech-free time.

Seeking Support

- **IT Professionals**: Reach out to IT support to streamline your tech setup or troubleshoot issues.
- **Online Communities**: Join online groups or forums that offer peer support and advice on software, tools, and best practices.
- **Training Resources**: Utilize online courses, tutorials, or help centers provided by tech companies.

** Tips*

Bookmarks help articles or guides for frequently encountered tech issues to save time.

6.5 NAVIGATING CAREER PROGRESSION REMOTELY

Advancing your career in a remote work environment presents unique challenges and opportunities. Without the traditional office setting, visibility and networking require new approaches, and demonstrating your value becomes even more critical. This section provides an overview of strategies to help you navigate career progression remotely, setting the stage for a deeper dive in Chapter 8. You'll learn how to maintain visibility, seek professional development opportunities, and effectively advocate for yourself to ensure your career thrives in a flexible work landscape.

Visibility and Communication

Regular Status Updates:

- Tell your manager and team leaders about your progress, accomplishments, and challenges.
- Utilize shared documents or project management tools to maintain transparency.

Routine Check-Ins:

- Schedule one-on-one meetings with managers for feedback, guidance, and goal alignment.

Team Meetings:

- Actively participate in team meetings, offering insights, updates, or assistance.

Tips

Frame updates positively and align them with team goals to maintain relevance.

Professional Development Opportunities

- **Online Learning Platforms**: Leverage platforms like LinkedIn Learning, Coursera, or Udemy for relevant courses.
- **Webinars and Workshops**: Attend virtual workshops and webinars to gain new insights and industry knowledge.
- **Internal Programs**: Explore internal programs like job shadowing or knowledge-sharing sessions.

Tips

Regularly allocate time for learning in your schedule to stay on track.

Networking Remotely

- **Virtual Events**: Participate in virtual industry events or conferences to connect with peers and thought leaders.
- **LinkedIn Engagement**: Engage with posts, join groups, and share your insights to build a solid professional presence.
- **Informational Interviews**: Reach out to colleagues and industry professionals for informal chats or coffee sessions.

Tips

Send follow-up messages to deepen connections and express gratitude for the advice received.

Advocating for Yourself

- **Prepare Data-Driven Evidence**: Present data, KPIs, or examples demonstrating your impact.
- **Performance Reviews**: Use performance reviews to highlight achievements, outline new goals, and request support.
- **Promotion Conversations**: Clearly articulate why you deserve advancement, highlighting alignment with company needs.

Tips

Document successes throughout the year to create a comprehensive portfolio before review meetings.

Visibility, communication, learning, and networking are crucial for career growth in a remote setting. Being proactive and strategic about these aspects will help you progress effectively while working flexibly.

CHAPTER 7
YOUR MENTAL AND EMOTIONAL WELL-BEING

Maintaining mental and emotional well-being is essential for flexible workers to stay effective. Here's how to manage these challenges:

7.1 THE PSYCHOLOGY OF WORKING REMOTELY

Transitioning to remote work involves more than a shift in physical location; it also requires a fundamental change in mindset. With remote work, working autonomously is a must and comes with a higher level of self-responsibility.

- **Autonomy**: Flexible work provides greater independence, empowering you to shape your daily routine. However, this freedom demands strong self-discipline.
- **Responsibility**: With more control over your schedule comes greater responsibility. Self-motivation

and proactive communication are key to staying accountable.

* Tips

Establish personal accountability systems, like checklists or rewards, to maintain momentum.

Impact on Identity and Self-Perception

Remote work changes how you perceive yourself and your role.

- **Reduced Physical Presence**: Without the visual affirmation of being in a busy office, it's easy to feel disconnected or unrecognized. This can impact your self-worth and create a sense of invisibility.
- **Role Definition**: Flexible work often blurs the lines between personal and professional life, which may lead to identity confusion.

* Tips

Celebrate your achievements regularly, even small milestones, to reinforce your contributions and stay motivated.

Coping Mechanisms

To tackle the psychological challenges of remote work:

- **Set Boundaries**: Clearly distinguish between work and leisure time using a consistent schedule or separate workspaces.

- **Maintain Social Connections**: Engage with colleagues through virtual coffee breaks or casual chats to reduce feelings of isolation.
- **Professional Support**: If feelings of disconnection persist, consider professional support from counselors or career coaches.

* Tips

Regularly remind yourself why you chose flexible work, focusing on the positives it brings to your lifestyle.

Positive Psychology Techniques

Incorporating positive psychology techniques can enhance your satisfaction and productivity.

- **Gratitude Practice**: Keep a daily gratitude journal to acknowledge positive experiences and achievements.
- **Strengths-Based Approach**: To build confidence, identify and apply your unique strengths to your daily tasks.
- **Mindfulness Exercises**: Incorporate mindfulness exercises like meditation or yoga to reduce stress and improve focus.

* Tips

Create a "joy list" of activities that make you happy, and integrate these into your day as rewards.

7.2 STRATEGIES FOR MANAGING REMOTE WORK ANXIETY

As we have already discussed previously, remote working brings with it some additional challenges to your mental health. Recognizing and identifying what triggers anxiety in remote work settings is the first step to being able to address these issues effectively.

- **Unclear Expectations**: When roles and expectations are vague, anxiety can arise from confusion about priorities.
- **Communication Issues**: The lack of non-verbal cues in virtual communication can lead to misunderstandings and heightened stress.
- **Workload Imbalance**: Feeling overwhelmed by workload or fearing underperformance can cause significant anxiety.

* Tips

Regular check-ins with your supervisor or team can clarify expectations and align priorities.

Creating a Supportive Environment

A supportive environment is critical to reducing remote work anxiety.

- **Open Communication**: Encourage a culture where discussing mental health challenges is normalized.

- **Team Support**: Facilitate team bonding and collaboration so everyone feels connected and valued.
- **Managerial Support**: Leaders should be approachable and proactive in providing emotional support.

* Tips

Create time and a designated space during team meetings for mental health discussions, making sharing concerns easier.

Practical Anxiety Management Techniques

Employ practical strategies to manage daily stress:

- **Time Management**: Use task prioritization techniques like the Eisenhower Box (section 3.2) to organize your day and minimize overwhelm.
- **Mindfulness Practices**: Simple breathing exercises or short meditation sessions can refocus and calm the mind.
- **Goal Setting**: Setting clear, achievable goals provides a sense of direction and accomplishment. (Refer to section 2.2 *Setting Personal and Professional Goals*)

* Tips

Break large tasks into manageable chunks, tackling one at a time to reduce pressure.

Professional Resources

If anxiety persists, consider seeking professional help.

- **Counselors and Therapists**: Virtual counseling can offer valuable strategies for managing work-related stress.
- **Employee Assistance Programs (EAPs)**: Check if your employer provides an EAP for mental health support.
- **Support Networks**: Peer support groups and mental health organizations can provide community and access to additional resources.

* Tips

Don't hesitate to reach out to trusted colleagues, family, or friends for emotional support.

Mindfulness and Meditation for Remote Workers

Practicing mindfulness can significantly improve your remote work experience.

- **Reduced Stress**: Mindfulness helps lower stress levels by encouraging you to focus on the present moment.
- **Improved Focus**: Meditation enhances concentration, enabling you to work more efficiently.
- **Greater Resilience**: Being present helps develop a positive outlook and builds resilience against challenges.

Tips

Start with a few minutes of meditation daily, gradually increasing over time.

Incorporating Mindfulness into the Workday

Simple ways to bring mindfulness into your workday:

- **Mindful Breathing**: Take deep breaths between tasks for 1-2 minutes to center yourself.
- **Meditation Breaks**: Short meditation breaks (5-10 minutes) between work intervals help clear your mind and reset your focus.
- **Body Scans**: Practice body scans to become aware of and release tension.

Tips:

Pair mindfulness practices with morning coffee or post-lunch break routines.

Mindfulness Apps and Resources

Explore these helpful apps and resources:

- **Headspace**: Offers guided meditations and mindfulness exercises.
- Calm: Features breathing exercises and relaxation techniques.
- **Insight Timer**: Provides access to thousands of guided meditations.

Tips

Experiment with different apps to find the one that best suits your needs.

Building a Regular Practice

To integrate mindfulness into your work routine:

- **Consistency**: Schedule regular meditation sessions, treating them as essential breaks.
- **Journaling**: Reflect on your mindfulness journey by journaling any positive changes.
- **Community**: Join mindfulness groups or forums to share progress and stay motivated.

Tips

Start small and be patient with your practice; consistency is more important than duration.

7.3 THE IMPACT OF PHYSICAL SPACE ON MENTAL HEALTH

Your physical workspace significantly influences your mental well-being and productivity. An organized, ergonomic, and aesthetically pleasing environment can enhance focus, reduce stress, and boost overall happiness. Conversely, a cluttered or poorly designed space can increase anxiety and decrease productivity. This section explores the connection between your physical surroundings and mental health, offering practical tips on optimizing your home office to create a supportive and uplifting atmosphere that promotes both efficiency and well-being.

Workspace Design

The design and setup of your home office significantly impact your mental health. (Refer to section 3.1, *Designing Your Ultimate Home Office*):

- **Lighting**: Natural light reduces stress and increases productivity. Position your desk near a window or use lamps that mimic daylight.
- **Ergonomics**: An ergonomic chair and desk setup prevent strain and promote good posture.
- **Personalization**: Add personal touches like photos or artwork to make the space feel inviting.

** Tips*

Adjust screen brightness and contrast to reduce eye strain, especially if you work long hours.

Separation of Spaces

Maintaining a clear boundary between work and personal spaces is crucial for mental well-being:

- **Dedicated Workspace**: To signal work mode, create a specific area for work, even if it's a small corner.
- **Visual Barriers**: Use curtains or room dividers to separate your work area if space is limited.

- **Clear Transitions:** Establish rituals like changing clothes or walking to transition between work and personal time.

Tips

Avoid bringing work into your living or sleeping areas to reinforce the separation.

Nature and Greenery

Incorporating nature into your workspace can boost mood and reduce stress:

- **Plants**: Houseplants like snake plants or pothos improve air quality and create a calming environment.
- **Natural Elements**: Include natural elements like stones, wood, or water features for added tranquility.
- **Scenery**: Position your desk with a view of the outdoors to refresh your mind.

Tips

Choose low-maintenance plants if you have a busy schedule or don't possess a green thumb.

Regular Changes and Refreshes

Making regular updates to your workspace can prevent monotony:

- **Rearrangement**: Rearrange furniture or décor periodically to create a sense of novelty.
- **New Colors**: Change color schemes using new accessories or desk items to refresh your environment.
- **Decluttering**: Declutter regularly to reduce distractions and enhance focus.

* Tips

Incorporate seasonal touches like flowers in spring or warm textiles in winter to match the changing seasons.

7.4 BUILDING A SUPPORT NETWORK FOR REMOTE WORK SUCCESS

A strong support network is essential for thriving in a remote work environment. Isolation and disconnection are common challenges for remote workers, making it crucial to foster relationships that provide professional support and personal camaraderie. This section delves into the importance of building a robust support network, offering strategies for connecting with colleagues, engaging in professional communities, and leveraging social and collaborative tools. Creating a reliable support system can enhance your remote work experience, gain valuable insights, and maintain a sense of community and belonging.

Leveraging Existing Networks

Utilize your current network for support and camaraderie:

- **Reconnect**: Reach out to former colleagues, friends, and acquaintances who understand your industry.

- **LinkedIn & Social Media**: Leverage LinkedIn or other professional networks to maintain relationships and seek advice.
- **Professional Associations**: Join associations relevant to your field to stay updated and connect with peers.

Tips

Regularly engage with your network by sharing updates or asking for feedback.

Engaging in Virtual Communities

Participate in virtual communities for advice and networking:

- **Forums & Groups**: Join forums like Reddit, Facebook Groups, or Slack communities dedicated to your profession.
- **Webinars & Meetups**: Attend webinars, online meetups, or virtual conferences to learn and connect with peers.
- **Resource Sharing**: Share resources, articles, or tools that can benefit others in the community.

Tips

Seek out diverse communities to broaden your knowledge and perspectives.

Creating Peer Groups

Form or join peer support groups:

- **Interest-Based Groups**: Join groups based on shared interests like technology, wellness, or productivity.
- **Accountability Partners**: Partner with someone who shares similar goals to motivate each other.
- **Regular Check-Ins**: Schedule recurring meetings to share progress, challenges, and insights.

** Tips*

Encourage group members to celebrate wins, no matter how small, to build morale.

Family and Household Support

Involve family and household members to build a supportive environment:

- **Mutual Respect**: Set clear work boundaries with family members to avoid interruptions.
- **Household Responsibilities**: Divide chores and responsibilities to minimize stress and distractions.
- **Encouragement**: Encourage positive reinforcement and understanding of each other's work challenges.

** Tips*

Create a family calendar to align schedules and plan for collaborative family time.

Emotional resilience is the backbone of successful flexible work. Building strategies around structure, self-care, and strong support networks will bolster your mental well-being and make remote work fulfilling.

CHAPTER 8
ADVANCING YOUR CAREER IN A FLEXIBLE WORLD

Advancing your career in a flexible work environment requires a strategic approach encompassing skill-building, networking, and effective personal branding. In this chapter, you'll learn how to identify and develop the skills necessary for career growth, build valuable connections in a virtual world, and find and secure new opportunities while working remotely. Whether you're aiming for a promotion within your current organization or exploring external opportunities, these insights and strategies will help you navigate the path to success.

8.1 SKILL-BUILDING AND CONTINUOUS LEARNING FROM HOME

Adopting a growth mindset is foundational for continuous learning and professional development. Embracing a proactive approach to professional development not only enhances your expertise but also opens up new opportunities for growth and innovation.

- **View Challenges as Opportunities**: Instead of seeing challenges as obstacles, view them as chances to expand your abilities and knowledge.
- **Learn from Feedback**: Welcome constructive criticism as a tool for learning, not a judgment of your capabilities.
- **Celebrate Effort, Not Just Success**: Recognize the effort you put into learning, regardless of the immediate outcomes.

Tips

Reflect on daily experiences to identify lessons and growth opportunities, even in routine tasks.

Identifying Skill Gaps

Understanding your current skills and identifying gaps are crucial steps in personal and professional growth.

- **Self-Assessment**: Regularly evaluate your skills against job requirements and industry trends.
- **Feedback from Others**: Seek feedback from colleagues, supervisors, or mentors to gain external perspectives on your skill set.
- **Industry Benchmarks**: Stay updated with industry standards to ensure your skills remain competitive.

Tips

Use professional competency frameworks or skill assessment tools available to your industry for a more structured analysis.

Online Learning Platforms

Numerous online platforms provide resources for skill development and professional growth.

- **MOOCs** (Massive Open Online Courses): Platforms like Coursera, edX, and Udemy offer courses from universities and industry leaders worldwide.
- **Webinars and Virtual Workshops**: Attend live webinars and workshops presented by professional associations, industry experts, or training organizations.
- **Subscription Services**: Services like LinkedIn Learning provide unlimited access to their course libraries for a monthly fee.

Tips

Choose courses with hands-on projects or case studies to apply your learning directly to real-world scenarios.

Creating a Personalized Learning Plan

Develop a structured approach to continuous learning tailored to your goals.

- **Define Clear Objectives**: Set specific, measurable goals for your current role and future career aspirations. (Refer to section 2.2 *Setting Personal and Professional Goals*)
- **Schedule Learning Time**: Allocate weekly time slots for learning activities to ensure consistency.

- **Diverse Learning Methods**: Combine theoretical learning with practical applications like simulations, real-life projects, or peer discussions.
- **Review and Adjust**: Review your learning plan's progress regularly, and be flexible about adjusting it as your goals evolve or new opportunities arise.

* Tips

Incorporate learning into your daily routine by listening to podcasts, reading industry articles, or discussing with peers during breaks.

8.2 NETWORKING AND COLLABORATION IN A VIRTUAL WORLD

Building and maintaining professional relationships virtually can enhance your career opportunities, provide support, and foster innovation. This section explores the strategies for thriving in a virtual world, from leveraging social media and attending virtual events to using collaboration tools that facilitate seamless teamwork.

Leveraging Social Media

Social media platforms, particularly LinkedIn, are invaluable for networking in today's digital age.

- **Optimize Your Profile**: Ensure your LinkedIn profile is complete and showcases your skills, experiences, and professional interests.

- **Share Insights and Content**: Regularly post articles, thoughts, and insights relevant to your industry to attract attention from peers and leaders.
- **Engage with Others**: Comment on, share, and react to posts by others in your network to increase visibility and engagement.

Tips

Use LinkedIn's feature to notify connections about career updates and achievements to keep your network informed and engaged.

Virtual Networking Events

Maximizing virtual networking events can expand your professional circle and open new opportunities.

- **Preparation**: Research attendees and speakers to identify who you want to connect with.
- **Engagement**: Participate actively during the event through Q&A sessions, breakout rooms, and chat features.
- **Follow-up**: Send personalized connection requests or emails to those you interacted with shortly after the event, mentioning specific discussions or shared interests.

Tips

Keep notes during the event to refer to in follow-ups, making your messages more personal and memorable.

Building a Collaborative Mindset

Fostering a collaborative mindset is crucial in a virtual environment.

- **Seek Opportunities for Partnership**: Find ways to collaborate on projects or initiatives that align with your skills and professional goals.
- **Share Resources and Knowledge**: Generously share your expertise and resources. This reciprocity often leads to mutual growth and learning.
- **Participate in Group Projects**: Join or initiate group projects that allow you to work with new individuals within your field.

* Tips

Always approach collaborations with a mindset of what you can contribute rather than what you can gain.

Maintaining and Nurturing Relationships

Building lasting professional relationships in a remote or virtual environment requires consistent effort.

- **Regular Communication**: Keep in touch with your contacts through periodic updates, sharing valuable resources, or simply checking in.
- **Virtual Coffee Chats**: Schedule informal chats with colleagues and peers to keep the relationship alive.
- **Show Appreciation**: Express gratitude when others assist you, offer guidance, or provide opportunities.

Tips

Utilize calendar reminders to follow up with key contacts every few months to ensure you maintain regular contact.

By strategically leveraging social media, actively participating in virtual networking events, developing a collaborative mindset, and nurturing relationships, you can effectively build and maintain a robust professional network in a virtual world.

8.3 PERSONAL BRANDING FOR THE REMOTE WORKER

In the world of flexible work, establishing a strong personal brand is more important than ever. Your personal brand represents your professional identity and helps differentiate you in a crowded marketplace. This section will delve into the essentials of personal branding for remote workers, offering insights on how to create a compelling online presence, communicate your unique value proposition, and consistently showcase your expertise. By cultivating a robust personal brand, you can enhance your visibility, build credibility, and attract new opportunities, ensuring continued growth and success in the flexible work landscape.

Defining Your Personal Brand

Your brand is the unique combination of your skills, values, and goals that set you apart.

- **Identify Core Values**: Reflect on your core values and beliefs that reflect what you stand for and align with your career aspirations.
- **Recognize Unique Strengths**: Pinpoint the unique skills and strengths that you bring to your industry or role.
- **Craft a Brand Statement**: Write a concise statement summarizing who you are professionally and what you aim to achieve.

* Tips

Regularly revisit your brand statement to ensure it stays relevant to your evolving career goals.

Online Presence and Visibility

A solid online presence is essential for building and maintaining your personal brand.

- **Social Media Profiles**: Optimize your social media profiles to reflect your brand, ensuring consistency in tone, imagery, and messaging.
- **Content Creation**: Share original content, such as articles, videos, or infographics, that aligns with your professional expertise and interests.
- **Engage with Others**: Comment on relevant industry posts and join discussions to demonstrate your knowledge and build credibility.

* Tips

Use a content calendar to plan and schedule your posts in advance, ensuring consistent engagement with your intended audience.

Authenticity in Branding

Authenticity is vital to building trust and credibility.

- **Showcase Real Achievements**: Highlight genuine projects, roles, and accomplishments that reflect your journey and skills.
- **Maintain Consistency**: Keep your messaging consistent across all platforms, from social media posts to emails and articles.
- **Be True to Yourself**: Authentically present yourself, avoiding the temptation to embellish or misrepresent.

* Tips

Ask colleagues or mentors for feedback on your brand messaging to ensure it aligns with how you're perceived.

Measuring Brand Impact

Regular assessment of your brand's impact allows you to refine your strategies.

- **Track Metrics**: Monitor relevant metrics, such as follower growth, engagement rates, and profile views.

- **Solicit Feedback**: Ask colleagues, mentors, and followers for their perception of your brand and suggestions for improvement.
- **Adjust Strategies**: Refine your content strategy, posting frequency, and messaging based on feedback and metrics.

* Tips

Periodically audit your online profiles and content to remove outdated information or posts that don't align with your brand.

By defining your personal brand, building a strong online presence, staying authentic, and regularly measuring impact, you'll effectively position yourself as a credible and influential professional in your field.

8.4 FINDING AND SECURING REMOTE WORK OPPORTUNITIES

Navigating the job market for remote roles requires tailored strategies highlighting your qualifications and adaptability to remote environments. Here's how to refine your approach from job search to negotiation.

Job Search Strategies

- **Niche Job Boards:** Focus on job boards specializing in remote opportunities, such as We Work Remotely, Remote.co, and FlexJobs, where employers are already attuned to the dynamics of remote work.

- **Remote-Friendly Company Directories:** Utilize directories like Remote OK and others that list companies open to remote work. This can help you target your applications more effectively.
- **Leverage LinkedIn:** Use LinkedIn to connect with hiring managers directly and follow companies for job openings and company culture updates.

Tips

Set up alerts on these platforms to be notified immediately of new openings in your field and desired location.

Application Customization

- **Highlight Remote Skills**: In your resume and cover letter, emphasize skills essential for remote work, such as self-motivation, communication, and proficiency with virtual collaboration tools.
- **Tailor Your Experiences**: Customize your application to reflect how your past experiences align with the remote role. Be specific about any remote work you have done and the tools you have used.
- **Keywords and Phrases**: Include keywords related to remote work from the job description, such as "virtual teamwork," "digital communication," or "independent project management."

Tips

Review each job description carefully and mirror their language when describing your experiences and skills.

Interview Preparation

- **Technical Setup**: Ensure your video conferencing software is up-to-date, your internet connection is stable, and your audio/video quality is clear.
- **Environment Considerations**: Choose a quiet, well-lit setting for the interview to minimize distractions and present a professional image.
- **Communicate Remote Work Competencies**: Be prepared to discuss how you handle time management, collaboration, and productivity challenges in a remote setting.

* Tips

Conduct a mock video interview with a friend to refine your setup and delivery.

Negotiating Remote Work Arrangements

- **Flexibility**: Discuss your need for flexible hours, if applicable, and how you plan to align your schedule with team goals and deadlines
- **Communicate Expectations**: Clarify how often you communicate with your team and supervisors through what channels.
- **Performance Metrics**: Talk about how your performance will be measured, ensuring the metrics are fair and attainable in a remote setting.

* Tips

Express your dedication to contributing positively to the team and ask for a trial period to demonstrate the effectiveness of the proposed work arrangement.

By implementing these strategies, you can enhance your visibility in the remote job market, tailor your applications to showcase your readiness for remote roles, prepare effectively for remote interviews, and negotiate terms that support a successful remote work career.

8.5 NAVIGATING PROMOTIONS AND RAISES AS A REMOTE EMPLOYEE

Securing promotions and raises in a flexible work environment requires a proactive approach. By clearly articulating your goals and demonstrating your value remotely, you can position yourself for advancement.

Setting and Communicating Career Goals

- **Define Clear Objectives**: Outline your desired career trajectory and the specific skills or roles you aim to achieve. (Refer to section 2.2 *Setting Personal and Professional Goals*)
- **Align with Management**: Regularly discuss your career goals with your supervisor to ensure your aspirations align with company needs.
- **Create a Development Plan**: Develop a plan that includes milestones and timelines, sharing it with your manager to gain support and guidance.

* Tips

Schedule regular check-ins with your manager to discuss your progress and adjust the plan as needed.

Demonstrating Your Value

Increase Visibility: Stay visible by participating actively in virtual meetings, contributing to team discussions, and sharing regular updates.

- **Record Achievements**: Record your accomplishments, including metrics and specific feedback highlighting your contributions.
- **Showcase Leadership**: Volunteer for projects demonstrating your leadership skills, such as mentoring new hires or leading virtual initiatives.

* Tips

Use internal communication channels to share team successes and highlight your role in achieving them.

Preparing for Performance Reviews

- **Evidence-Based Preparation**: Gather data on your key achievements, project outcomes, and how you contributed to team goals. Collect positive feedback from colleagues and clients.
- **Align with Company Goals**: Frame your accomplishments in the context of the company's

strategic objectives to show how your contributions align with broader goals.
- **Self-Assessment**: Conduct a self-assessment to identify areas for improvement and include these in your review to demonstrate a proactive approach to growth.

* Tips

Create a one-pager summarizing your achievements, challenges, and future goals to streamline the review discussion.

Negotiation Strategies

- **Market Standards**: Research industry salary standards and compare your current role to similar roles in the market to support your request.
- **Results-Based Case**: Present a case based on your results and impact on the company. Highlight specific projects where your contributions directly influenced positive outcomes.
- **Timing Matters**: Choose a time to negotiate when the company is financially stable or growing and your recent achievements are fresh. Avoid negotiating during a period of high organizational uncertainty.

* Tips

Prepare counter-arguments to potential objections that management may raise and be ready to propose compromises.

By setting clear career goals, consistently demonstrating your value, and thoroughly preparing for performance reviews, you'll be well-positioned to negotiate promotions and raises that recognize your contributions as a remote employee.

CHAPTER 9
FUTURE-PROOFING YOUR REMOTE WORK LIFE

In an ever-changing work landscape, future-proofing your remote work life is crucial. Rapid technological advancements and shifting economic trends demand proactive preparation to ensure continued growth and success. This chapter explores what flexible workers should anticipate and adapt to, emphasizing how they can remain resilient by embracing new technologies, adopting sustainable practices, and securing their financial future.

9.1 ANTICIPATING AND ADAPTING TO CHANGES IN REMOTE WORK

To thrive in this environment, it's essential to anticipate and adapt to technological advancements and shifting workplace changes proactively. This section explores strategies for staying informed about emerging trends, developing an adaptive mindset, and continuously refining your skills.

Staying Informed Keep up-to-date with the latest trends and shifts in remote work by following industry news, reading reports, and listening to thought leaders. Staying informed allows you to foresee changes in the job market and adapt quickly.

Adaptive Mindset Cultivate a mindset that embraces change and seeks innovative solutions. Adaptability means letting go of outdated processes and adopting new technologies and strategies.

Continuous Skill Development Commit to learning and improving your skills regularly. Whether through formal courses, certifications, or self-directed learning, continuous skill development ensures you're always equipped with relevant and competitive expertise.

Scenario Planning Engage in scenario planning by imagining future work environments and assessing how they could affect your career. Prepare adaptable strategies and flexible plans for each scenario, ensuring you're ready for whatever comes next.

* Tips

Set aside dedicated time each week to focus on skill development or trend research and identify any gaps in your current capabilities that you can work on closing.

9.2 THE ROLE OF AI AND AUTOMATION IN FLEXIBLE WORK

Artificial intelligence (AI) and automation are transforming the landscape of flexible work, offering tools and technologies that enhance productivity and efficiency. Understanding and leveraging these advancements can give remote workers a significant advantage. This section explores how AI and automation can streamline workflows, assist in decision-making, and free up time for more strategic tasks.

Understanding Artificial Intelligence (AI) and Automation

AI and automation technologies are designed to handle repetitive, time-consuming tasks, allowing employees to focus on more complex and strategic activities. AI can analyze vast amounts of data quickly and accurately, providing insights that support decision-making and problem-solving. Automation tools, meanwhile, can manage routine processes such as data entry, scheduling, and communication, significantly reducing the administrative burden on workers.

Impact on Tasks, Roles, and Skills Integration of AI and automation is reshaping job roles and the skills required for success. Routine tasks are increasingly automated, meaning workers must develop skills in areas such as data analysis, critical thinking, and complex problem-solving. Roles are evolving to focus more on managing and interpreting automated outputs, rather than performing manual tasks.

Streamlining Workflows AI and automation can streamline workflows by optimizing processes and reducing the time needed to complete tasks. For example:

- **Automated Scheduling**: Tools like AI-powered calendars can automatically schedule meetings, considering participants' availability and preferences.

- **Data Management**: AI can sort, analyze, and interpret large datasets, providing actionable insights without manual intervention.
- **Customer Service**: Chatbots and virtual assistants can handle customer inquiries, freeing up human agents to tackle more complex issues.

Assisting in Decision-Making AI enhances decision-making by providing data-driven insights and predictive analytics. For instance:

- **Predictive Analysis**: AI can predict market trends, customer behavior, and potential risks, helping businesses make informed decisions.
- **Personalized Recommendations**: AI systems can analyze user behavior to offer personalized suggestions, improving customer satisfaction and engagement.

Freeing Up Time for Strategic Tasks By automating routine activities, AI and automation free up valuable time for workers to focus on strategic and creative tasks. This shift enables remote workers to:

- **Innovate and Create**: With more time available, employees can engage in brainstorming, innovation, and creative problem-solving.
- **Strategic Planning**: Workers can dedicate more effort to long-term planning and strategy development, enhancing overall business performance.

- **Skill Development**: Extra time allows continuous learning and skill enhancement, ensuring workers remain competitive in a rapidly evolving job market.

Embracing Technology Embracing these technologies allows remote workers to focus on higher-value activities, driving both personal and organizational growth. Understanding and leveraging AI and automation is important for staying ahead. Embrace technological changes rather than resist them. Adapt to new technologies that enhance your productivity and also ensure you remain relevant and competitive in your field. Here's how you can effectively embrace these advancements:

Upskill in AI and Automation

- **Learn New Software**: Stay updated with the latest software that incorporates AI and automation. For instance, familiarize yourself with AI tools such as ChatGPT, Google Gemini, Microsoft Copilot or specific project management software enhanced with AI features, automated data analysis tools, or customer relationship management (CRM) systems that use AI for predictive insights.
- **Master Emerging Tools**: Dedicate time to mastering emerging tools and platforms relevant to your industry. This could include anything from AI-powered marketing tools to automated accounting systems to advanced analytics platforms.

Practical Steps to Upskill

- **Online Courses**: Enroll in courses focusing on AI, machine learning, and automation. Platforms like Coursera, Udemy, and LinkedIn Learning offer specialized courses designed to enhance your skills in these areas.
- **Certifications**: Obtain AI and automation tools certifications to validate your expertise and make you more marketable. Certifications from recognized institutions or tech companies can significantly boost your resume.
- **Practical Application**: Apply your knowledge by incorporating new tools into your daily workflow. Experiment with AI features in your current software, automate repetitive tasks, and seek out projects that allow you to utilize these new skills.
- **Continuous Learning**: Technology is always evolving, so commit to continuous learning. Follow industry blogs, join professional networks, and attend webinars and conferences to stay ahead of the curve.

* Tips

Experiment with AI tools in your daily work to identify those that complement your tasks and enhance productivity. Test drive some of these tools where possible. Many of these tools are available for a limited trial or free with limitations.

The more familiar you become with these tools, the better you adapt to technological shifts. You also position yourself as a forward-thinking professional ready to leverage technological advancements. This enhances your current performance and better prepares you for future opportunities.

9.3 SUSTAINABLE REMOTE WORK PRACTICES

Adopting sustainable remote work practices is more than just maintaining productivity, it's about creating a balanced and healthy work environment that supports your physical and mental health. This section explores practical ways to integrate sustainability into your remote work routine, covering aspects such as ergonomic workspace setup, eco-friendly practices, and strategies to maintain a healthy work-life balance.

Work-Life Balance Reiterate that a healthy work-life balance is crucial to long-term sustainability. Encourage setting clear boundaries for work hours, practicing self-care, and finding time for hobbies or activities that rejuvenate the mind.

Eco-Friendly Home Office Share practical tips for building an eco-friendly workspace. This could include switching to energy-efficient lighting, reducing paper use by going digital and sourcing sustainable office supplies.

Mental Health Strategies Provide long-term mental health strategies. Encourage regular check-ins with mental health professionals, practice mindfulness techniques like meditation or yoga, and incorporate digital detoxes to limit screen time and technology dependence. (Refer to Chapter 7, *Your Mental and Emotional Well-being*).

Community Engagement Highlight the significance of staying engaged with local or professional communities to counteract the isolation that sometimes accompanies remote work. This can include participating in local events, volunteering, or joining virtual interest groups.

Tips

Consider joining neighborhood sustainability initiatives or professional groups. These groups provide a sense of community and help you stay informed about new ways to improve sustainability at home or in your professional network.

Implementing these sustainable practices can ensure a more harmonious and effective remote work experience. This is essential for your long-term success and well-being.

9.4 BALANCING FLEXIBILITY WITH SECURITY: FINANCIAL PLANNING FOR THE FUTURE

As we have discussed, remote work offers unparalleled flexibility. But it's also important to balance this freedom with financial security. Proper financial planning ensures you can enjoy the benefits of a flexible work environment without compromising your long-term stability. This section provides strategies for diversifying income streams, planning for retirement, and securing appropriate insurance coverage.

Financial Planning for Remote Workers

Consider the irregular income patterns of flexible work and set up an emergency fund that covers at least six months of living expenses.

Tips

Use a high-yield savings account to store your emergency fund, offering liquidity and earning better interest.

Diversifying Income Streams

Explore freelance projects, passive income sources (e.g., content royalties, affiliate marketing), and investments to broaden your income base.

Tips

Invest in skills that can lead to high-demand, side-gig opportunities, such as graphic design, copywriting, or web development.

Retirement Planning

Prioritize long-term savings by opening an Individual Retirement Account (IRA) and automating regular contributions. Consider diversifying investments into stocks, bonds, or real estate.

Tips

Take advantage of online retirement planning tools to visualize and plan various retirement scenarios.

Insurance Considerations

Ensure comprehensive protection with health insurance, professional liability insurance (to cover work-related errors), and home office insurance (for equipment and supplies).

*Tips

Compare quotes from different insurers and bundle policies to save on premiums.

Being prepared for the future of remote work means you can navigate changes smoothly, seize new opportunities, and maintain a competitive edge in your career. If you anticipate future changes, adopt AI and automation, prioritize sustainable work practices, and secure your finances, you can effectively future-proof your remote work life and remain adaptable in an unpredictable world.

CHAPTER 10
BEYOND THE HOME OFFICE

This chapter explores the broader aspects of maintaining a balanced and fulfilling lifestyle while working remotely. A healthy work-life balance has numerous benefits, impacting productivity, professional success, and personal satisfaction and well-being. Here, we'll delve into various activities and strategies that can enrich your life outside the confines of your home office, ensuring that you thrive in both your professional and personal spheres.

10.1 INTEGRATING WORK AND LIFE: A HOLISTIC APPROACH

A holistic approach means blending work and personal life to enrich both. It's about finding a rhythm where career goals are met while nurturing personal relationships and hobbies. Instead of striving for a strict balance, embrace seamless integration where work and life activities can complement and support one another. For instance, flexible hours can be used to manage and balance family needs or personal pursuits alongside work commitments.

Mindfulness in Daily Activities Practicing mindfulness is key to successful integration. Whether working on a project or spending time with family, being fully present ensures engagement and fulfillment from each moment. Techniques like mindful breathing or meditation breaks can help with this.

Setting Integrated Goals Set goals that encompass professional achievements and personal well-being. For instance, aim for a successful project launch while dedicating time to family activities or hobbies. Pursuing fulfillment in every area helps build a more satisfying lifestyle.

* Tips

Create a daily or weekly schedule that includes time for work tasks, hobbies, family activities, and self-care, ensuring you consistently nurture every aspect of your life.

10.2 HOBBIES AND INTERESTS: RECHARGING OUTSIDE WORK HOURS

Hobbies can bring psychological and physical benefits. They provide a creative outlet that reduces stress and enhances productivity. Whether a craft project or an outdoor activity, these pastimes recharge your mental batteries. Certain hobbies are particularly effective for stress relief. Gardening, painting, playing musical instruments, or even puzzle-solving are all excellent options. Give yourself permission to play and unwind. Hobbies can foster social interaction and reduce the isolation often felt with remote work. Join a club, take a class, or participate in group activities to connect with others who share your interests and build a supportive community.

Finding Your Passion

- If you are still unsure where to start, explore activities that align with your personal interests. Reflect on what excites or inspires you, then experiment with various hobbies to see which resonate. Schedule regular sessions to make time for them in your routine.

* Tips

Dedicate a fixed amount of time each week to hobbies or interests, treating this as a non-negotiable appointment with yourself to recharge and nurture your creativity.

10.3 VOLUNTEERING AND COMMUNITY ENGAGEMENT AS A REMOTE WORKER

Benefits of Volunteering Volunteering offers numerous benefits. It helps develop new skills, expands networks, and provides emotional fulfillment by giving back. It can also build a sense of purpose and strengthen social connections.

Finding Remote Volunteering Opportunities Many organizations now offer remote volunteering roles, making it easy to contribute regardless of location. Websites like VolunteerMatch and Catchafire can connect you to opportunities aligned with your skills and interests.

Engaging with Local Communities Beyond remote options, consider local community engagement. Join neighborhood clean-up projects, participate in local events, or volunteer at nearby shelters. It fosters a sense of belonging and helps counter remote workers' isolation.

Volunteering as Professional Development Volunteering can also enhance your career by offering leadership opportunities and team projects, helping you develop new skills outside your regular role. Whether organizing events or managing initiatives, volunteering builds experience that can translate into professional growth.

* Tips

Make volunteering an extension of your professional journey by seeking roles where you can apply and expand your existing skill set. Treat it like any other opportunity—prepare, deliver value, and document your achievements.

10.4 PHYSICAL WELLNESS AND NUTRITION FOR THE HOME-BASED WORKER

Physical health is crucial to productivity and overall satisfaction. A robust and well-nourished body supports mental clarity and helps you tackle work with enthusiasm and energy.

Exercise Routines for Remote Workers:

- Embrace exercise routines that blend seamlessly into your schedule. Consider quick home workouts like bodyweight exercises, yoga, or stretching. Outdoor activities like walking or jogging provide fresh air and a change of scenery while keeping you active. (Refer to section 3.4, *Establishing a Powerful Daily Routine*, and section 3.5, *The Role of Physical Fitness to Enhance Productivity*)

Nutritional Wellness:

- Maintain a balanced diet to stay energized. Plan meals to ensure they're nutritious and easy to prepare. Stock up on healthy snacks like nuts, fruits, and yogurt to avoid eating processed junk food. Stay hydrated with plenty of water throughout the day.

Ergonomic Health Practices:

- Set up your workspace ergonomically to minimize strain and injuries. Ensure your chair, desk, and monitor are positioned for good posture. Take regular movement breaks—stretch, walk around, or do light exercises to avoid sitting too long. (Refer to section 3.1 *Designing Your Ultimate Home Office*)

* Tips

Schedule physical activities like any other meeting or task in your calendar. This ensures you prioritize your health while balancing work and personal responsibilities.

10.5 PLANNING FOR TIME OFF: VACATIONS AND STAYCATIONS FOR THE FLEXIBLE WORKER

Regular time off prevents burnout and rejuvenates your mind and body. Make a habit of planning breaks so you can return to work refreshed and energized.

Planning Effective Vacations:

- When planning vacations, prioritize complete disconnection from work. Set clear boundaries with your team, delegate tasks, and ensure that work-related notifications are turned off during your break.
- Opt for destinations or activities that bring you joy and help you unwind.

Staycation Ideas for Remote Workers:

- A staycation can be just as refreshing as traveling far. Explore local attractions you've always wanted to visit, indulge in home spa days, take on creative projects like painting or writing, or have a movie marathon. Customize the experience to your interests while saving on travel costs.

Maximizing time Off:

- Plan your Time off in advance to ensure a smooth transition out of work. Automate or delegate tasks where possible, and communicate your absence to colleagues. On your return, ease back in by prioritizing tasks and allowing time for catch-up.

Tips

Schedule a "buffer day" before returning to work. Use this day to unwind from your vacation, review emails, and plan your first day back. This will help you transition smoothly and avoid post-vacation overwhelm.

Engaging in activities and interests outside your home office is not just a luxury but a necessity for maintaining overall health and mental well-being. Pursuing hobbies, volunteering, and staying physically active provide essential breaks from work demands, allowing you to recharge and gain new perspectives. These pursuits foster creativity, reduce stress, and enhance your sense of fulfillment, ultimately contributing to a more balanced and satisfying life. By prioritizing outside interests, you create a sustainable work-life dynamic supporting your professional success and personal happiness.

CHAPTER 11
WORKING FROM HOME FOR PARENTS

Working from home offers a unique set of benefits and challenges for parents. Balancing professional responsibilities with parenting requires careful planning, flexibility, and a supportive environment. Understanding the specific challenges associated with managing children of different age groups—infants, toddlers, children, and teenagers—can help parents develop effective strategies for creating a harmonious work-life balance. This chapter explores the benefits and pitfalls of remote work for parents and provides practical tips to manage both roles effectively.

11.1 BENEFITS AND PITFALLS

The flexibility of working from home allows parents to spend more time with their kids, witness important milestones, and better manage family commitments. However, it also presents significant pitfalls, such as frequent interruptions, balancing work and childcare duties, and the risk of blurred boundaries between professional and personal life. This section delves into these benefits and pitfalls, providing insights and strategies to help parents.

Benefits

- **Flexibility**: Working from home allows parents to adjust their work schedules around their children's needs, such as school runs, medical appointments, and extracurricular activities.
- **Increased Family Time**: Parents can spend more time with their children, witnessing milestones and participating in daily activities.
- **Reduced Commuting Stress**: Eliminating the daily commute saves time and energy, which can then be redirected towards the family or personal well-being.
- **Cost Savings**: By working from home, parents can save on childcare, transportation, and work-related expenses.

Pitfalls

- **Distractions and Interruptions**: Home environments can be filled with distractions, making it challenging to focus on work tasks.
- **Overlapping Boundaries**: Without a clear separation between work and home life, parents may struggle to switch off from work, leading to potential burnout.
- **Isolation**: Remote work can lead to feelings of isolation from colleagues and professional networks, which can impact career growth and personal well-being.

- **Childcare Challenges**: Balancing work demands with the needs of young children can be particularly challenging, requiring constant attention and intervention.

11.2. CHALLENGES OF MANAGING DIFFERENT AGE GROUPS

As a parent, managing children of different age groups while working from home presents its own set of challenges. Infants need constant care, toddlers demand supervision and engagement, school-aged children require educational support, and teenagers seek independence but still benefit from guidance. In this section, we will explore the unique needs and challenges of each age group and offer strategies that support both productive work and attentive parenting.

Infants (0-18 months)

- **Constant Attention**: Infants require constant care and attention, making it challenging to maintain uninterrupted work periods. Parents may need to schedule work around nap times or enlist the help of a partner or caregiver.
- **Unpredictable Schedules**: Infants' feeding and sleeping schedules can be unpredictable, requiring parents to remain flexible and adapt their work routines accordingly.
- **Sleep Management**: Balancing sleep for both the infant and the parent is crucial. Utilize tools like baby monitors to work while the infant sleeps in another room.

Toddlers (18 months to 3 years)

- **High Energy Levels:** Toddlers are active and curious, needing supervision and engagement in activities to keep them occupied.
- **Routine Establishment**: Setting up a structured routine with designated playtimes and quiet times can help manage their energy and provide parents with focused work periods.
- **Safe Play Areas**: Create secure, contained play areas where toddlers can explore without constant supervision.

Children (4 to 12 years)

- **Educational Needs**: School-aged children may require help with homework or supervision during remote learning sessions, which adds to their parents' responsibilities.
- **Engagement Activities**: Plan engaging activities that children can do independently, such as crafts, reading, or educational games.
- **After-School Routine**: Establish a routine that balances schoolwork, play, and downtime to ensure children remain productive and entertained.

Teenagers (13 to 19 years)

- **Independence**: Teenagers are generally more independent, allowing parents to focus more on work. However, they may still need support with schoolwork or emotional issues.

- **Screen Time Management**: Balancing screen time for teens, who may be engaged in online learning or social activities, is essential to ensuring their productivity and balance in their daily routines.
- **Emotional Support**: Provide emotional support and be available for meaningful conversations to help teens navigate the complexities of adolescence.

11.3 TIPS FOR PARENTS WORKING FROM HOME OR PERFORMING HYBRID WORK

Balancing flexible work with family responsibilities is a challenge that many parents face. Here are some practical tips to help parents create a productive and harmonious work-from-home or hybrid work environment:

Setting Boundaries with Family

Establishing boundaries with your family members ensures that everyone respects your work time.

- **Dedicated Workspace**: Designate a separate workspace, even if it's a corner of a room, that signals "work mode."
- **Communication**: Discuss your work hours openly with your family and the importance of minimizing interruptions.
- **Visual Cues**: Hang a sign on the doorknob, close the door, or wear headphones to visually cue others that you're in work mode and not to be disturbed.

Tips:

- Create a family calendar outlining your work hours and important meetings.
- Involve older children in setting expectations to give them a sense of responsibility.

Creating a Flexible Schedule A flexible schedule helps parents to work more effectively while managing childcare and family needs.

- **Core Work Hours**: Identify the most productive hours for focused work when your children are occupied (e.g., school time, nap time).
- **Split Shifts**: Split your workday into shifts: early morning or late night, with breaks during the day for family.
- **Tag-Team Parenting**: Coordinate shifts with your partner or a family member for uninterrupted work periods. If grandparents can help care for your children, set a mutually agreeable schedule for all parties but consider their health, energy levels, and mobility issues.
- **Use Childcare**: Arrange for childcare even while working from home to maintain productivity during core work hours.

Tips:

Set a realistic to-do list, prioritizing tasks that align with your productivity peaks.

- Use a planner to map out your work hours, family commitments, and personal breaks.

Engaging Children Constructively Keeping children engaged with activities helps maintain their well-being and gives parents uninterrupted work time.

- **Independent Play**: Provide age-appropriate toys, puzzles, or art supplies to occupy them.
- **Educational Activities**: Invest in educational apps, books, or virtual classes that stimulate learning.
- **Rewards System**: Create a simple rewards chart to incentivize good behavior or following instructions.

* Tips

- Organize a daily activity schedule with play, education, and downtime.
- Arrange virtual playdates or storytime sessions with family or friends.

Self-Care for Parents

Remembering to prioritize your well-being will enable you to support your family and perform at your best.

- **Scheduled Breaks**: Plan breaks for a short walk, meditation, or simply stepping away from the screen.
- **Social Support**: Connect with other parents in similar situations for shared advice or virtual social time.

- **Mindfulness Practices**: Practice mindfulness techniques like breathing exercises or journaling to manage stress.

* Tips

- Delegate age-appropriate chores to children to lighten your load.
- Don't hesitate to ask for help from family or seek childcare assistance.

Be Transparent with Your Employer

- Communicate openly with your manager about your home situation and any support you need to be effective.

By understanding the specific challenges of managing children of different age groups and implementing practical strategies, working parents can successfully navigate the complexities of remote work, ensuring both productivity and a nurturing home environment. The insights and techniques discussed in this chapter (and the rest of this book) are not just theoretical—they are practical, tested approaches that can make a significant difference in your daily life.

Embracing these strategies will help you create a more structured and harmonious household where your professional responsibilities and children's needs are met. By setting clear boundaries, developing a flexible yet consistent schedule, and leveraging the tools and resources available to you, you can reduce stress and enhance your overall well-being.

Moreover, fostering an environment where your children feel engaged and supported while you work can lead to a more fulfilling family life. When you successfully balance work and parenting, you model important skills like time management, adaptability, and resilience for your children. This benefits your career and contributes to your children's development and your family's happiness.

Implementing these strategies requires effort and consistency, but the rewards are substantial. You'll find yourself more focused and productive in your work while also being more present and attentive to your family. This dual success is the essence of a balanced, flexible work-life—one where professional and personal satisfaction go hand in hand.

Take the first step today by applying the techniques we've discussed. Adjust and refine them to suit your unique situation, and don't hesitate to seek additional support or resources as needed. Your journey to mastering remote work while raising children is an ongoing process, but with dedication and the right approach, you can achieve a harmonious and productive home environment.

Remember, you have the tools and the capability to succeed. Embrace these strategies, and watch as your work and family life transform for the better. The path to a balanced, fulfilling life is within your reach—start today and make the most of your flexible work arrangement.

THANK YOU FOR YOUR HELP!

Now that you have everything you need to navigate your way through the world of flexible work, it's time to pass on your newfound knowledge and show other readers where they can find the same help.

Leaving your honest opinion of this book on Amazon will guide other readers to the information they're looking for and help them find fulfilling and satisfying careers in flexible work.

Thank you for your help. The joys of working in this new world are kept alive when we pass on our knowledge – and you're helping me do just that.

Please leave your review on Amazon using the below QR code :

CONCLUSION

EMBRACE THE FLEXIBILITY

As you close the pages of Flex Appeal: Navigating the New World of Flexible Work, take a moment to reflect on the journey you've undertaken through this guide. You now have a deeper understanding of the nuances, challenges, and rewards of flexible work. From establishing clear boundaries and managing anxiety to networking remotely and future-proofing your career, the principles shared in this book are designed to help you thrive in this evolving landscape.

Working from home, especially with children, presents unique challenges and opportunities. Embracing the strategies outlined in this book will enable you to create a productive and nurturing home environment. Here's a recap of how these strategies can benefit you and why it's crucial to take action immediately:

Establish Clear Boundaries: Setting clear boundaries between work and home life is essential. This helps reduce stress, prevent burnout, and ensure that you are present for both your professional duties and your family. Implementing designated work hours and creating a separate workspace can drastically improve your focus and efficiency.

Master Time Management: Effective time management is a cornerstone of successful flexible work. Utilize techniques like time blocking, prioritizing tasks, and setting realistic goals to enhance productivity. This will also allow you to allocate quality time for your children, ensuring they feel supported and engaged.

Leverage Technology: Harness the power of technology to communicate effectively and nurture strong virtual teams. Project management software, video conferencing, and collaborative platforms can streamline your workflow and keep you connected with your colleagues.

Adopt Continuous Learning and Adaptability: The world of work is continuously evolving. Stay ahead by embracing a mindset of continuous learning and adaptability. Seek out new skills, stay open to opportunities, and be prepared to adjust your approach as needed.

Integrate Work and Life: Strive for a harmonious work-life integration that aligns with your personal and professional aspirations. Pursue hobbies, engage in physical wellness activities, and ensure you take regular breaks to recharge.

Build a Supportive Network: Engaging with a supportive community can mitigate feelings of isolation and provide professional development opportunities. Join online forums, attend virtual meetups, and connect with peers with similar challenges and goals.

Flexible work can transform your career and personal growth in incredible ways. By adopting these flexible practices, you can find greater job satisfaction, improve your mental and physical health, and unlock significant opportunities for advancement. The strategies outlined throughout this book aim to empower you to design a work-life setup that aligns with your professional goals and personal values. Whether you're seeking to build meaningful virtual connections, avoid burnout, or plan for the long term, this guide provides a toolkit for developing a career that fulfills and sustains you.

Remember, the journey towards achieving flexible work mastery is ongoing. Trends will shift, technologies will advance, and your circumstances may change. Embrace a mindset of continuous learning and adaptability. Seek out new skills, stay open to new opportunities, and don't hesitate to revise your approach as needed. By approaching this journey with positivity, resilience, and strategic action, you can create a work arrangement that brings fulfillment, happiness, and success.

The flexible work journey is exciting and transformational, offering enhanced happiness, fulfillment, and achievement opportunities. Embrace this path confidently, and let your unique skills and aspirations shine. I look forward to hearing about your journey and celebrating your success as you redefine the future of work! You can connect with me by email at *desmond.s.winters@gmail.com*.

Your voice matters! If you found this book valuable, please leave a review on Amazon. Your feedback helps other readers find practical guidance and empowers them to succeed in their flexible work journey. By sharing your insights and reflections, you support the author and contribute to a larger community of professionals navigating this exciting new world.

Thank you for joining me on this journey, and here's to your continued success as you navigate your flexible work path with confidence and clarity.

ABOUT THE AUTHOR

Desmond Miller is a seasoned business coach with a wealth of knowledge and experience. Over the past six years, he has dedicated himself to coaching, focusing on mastering the intricacies of remote work in the last three years. Desmond's diverse career spans multiple industries, including financial services, professional services, IT, building and construction, and education and training. In a career spanning over 40 years, he has held various roles from middle management to senior executive positions, and operated a number of small businesses, providing him with a well-rounded perspective on the challenges and opportunities within different sectors.

Continuous learning has been a cornerstone of Desmond's professional journey. His commitment to personal and professional growth drives his desire to help clients achieve their fullest potential. His extensive industry experience, combined with his hands-on coaching approach, equips him with the tools to share valuable insights and practical strategies with those he mentors.

Aside from his professional life, Desmond is a dedicated family man with one daughter. While he is typically based in Australia, he now enjoys the flexibility of traveling and working across Southeast Asia. In his free time, Desmond indulges in his love for travel, tennis, pickleball, and various creative pursuits.

www.ingramcontent.com/pod-product-compliance
Lightning Source LLC
Chambersburg PA
CBHW071456220526
45472CB00003B/817